We Are CODA

COPYRIGHT

Copyright ©Madeleine Hempstead October 2024.

Published: October 2024 Ladey Adey Publications, Ancaster, Lincolnshire UK.

Madeleine Hempstead has asserted her right to be identified as the author of this Work in accordance with the Copyright, Designs and Patents Act 1988.

ISBN: 978-1-913579-75-3 (Paperback).

ISBN: 978-1-913579-76-0 (E-Publication).

All rights reserved. No part of this publication may be reproduced, stored in a retrieval system, or transmitted in any form or by any means - for example, electronic, photocopy, recording - without the prior written permission of the publisher. The only exception is brief quotations in printed reviews.

British Library Cataloguing-in-Publication Data.

A catalogue record for this book is available from The British Library.

Cover Design by Abbirose Adey, of Ladey Adey Publications.

Cartoons & Caricatures by Chris Ryder, Witty Pics Ltd.

Neither the author nor the publisher can be held responsible for any loss, claim or damage arising out of the use, or misuse of the suggestions made, the failure to take business, financial or legal advice or for any material on third party websites.

The author and publisher has made every effort to ensure the external websites included in this book are correct and up to date at the time of going to press. The author and publisher are not responsible for the content, quality or continuing accessibility of the sites.

If you have enjoyed this book please give a review on Amazon® for Madeleine.

We Are CODA

Keeping the Connection Between
the Deaf and Hearing Worlds

Madeleine Hempstead

This memoir is based on my recollection of events, many long past. They may not always be exactly as others recall them. I acknowledge the family stories from our childhood and sibling discussions may not always be agreed upon by every member of the family. This reflects hindsight bias and how stories evolve and develop through oral retelling, especially amongst siblings.
Any mistakes are my own.

Dedication

to Mummy and Daddy

to my Sisters and Brothers

to Sebastian and Dominique

to Bella, Theodore, Etta,
Tilda and Lula

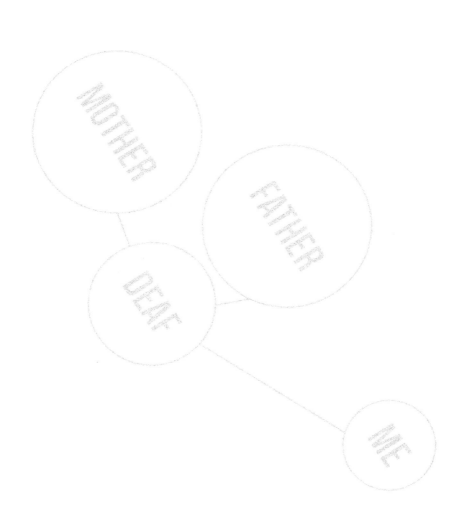

Contents

Foreword - Dr Neil J Alderman ix

Publisher's Note - Ladey Adey xi

Prologue - CODA: The Film xvii

Introduction 1

What's In A Sign Name? 7

My CODA Siblings 17

    Gabrielle 25

    Shaun..35

    Nickolas 37

    Josette 39

    Bernadette...45

    Eileen..49

    Madeleine..51

    Julian..65

    Claudius 67

    Francesca 71

My Deaf Parents...75

    Mummy 77

    Daddy 101

Extended Family...125

    Auntie Maureen 127

    Billy Evans 129

    Linda Fincham..132

    Paul Sibellas..135

    Sebastian 137

    Dominique 141

    Rachael and Michelle 144

Deaf Stories 147

My CODA Life 181

    Education and Employment 183

vii

We Are CODA

A Bicultural and Bilingual World 201
Travelling as a CODA 215
My First Non-Family CODA Experience.. 229

My CODA Future **233**
Where I Am Now 235

Extras.. **239**
Additional Reading 241
References 243

Appendices **247**
Appendix 1: Education for Deaf Prisoners 248
Appendix 2: British Sign Language Fingerspelling Alphabet 251

Acknowledgements... **253**

Index... **257**

Notes **261**

Endorsements **271**

Foreword
Dr Neil J Alderman

When asked by Madeleine Hempstead to write the foreword of her book *We Are CODA*, I felt privileged to do so. Her family was certainly unique. Her Deaf parents, William and Eileen Hempstead, had ten children all born hearing. In short, a staggering ten CODAs belonging to the same set of parents - a feat that is most likely to be unequalled elsewhere.

Being a born-Deaf person myself and starting my new job as a postdoctoral researcher at the Department of Chemical Engineering, University of Cambridge in 1982, I decided to join the Cambridge Deaf Club. It was there that the Deaf folk including William and Eileen Hempstead made me so very welcome. Doing some work on the Club's archives recently, I found the register of the Deaf and Dumb in Cambridge and elsewhere kept by Harry Rowland (who was himself Deaf) when he was the missioner from 1921 to 1957. This register revealed that many of the Deaf folk at the Club including William went to the same school as I did - Royal School for Deaf Children, Margate!

In the telling of the life story of William and Eileen, this book also gives memories from their children to what it is like being a CODA in terms of their experiences and frustrations that are so different from what is the norm. The love, gaiety and laughter of this close family is clearly manifested throughout the book. Madeleine must be congratulated in writing of this book with such honesty.

For those wanting to know more to what is like to be a CODA, I highly recommend this 'hard to be put down' book.

Dr Neil J Alderman

Publisher's Note
Ladey Adey

Madeleine's book has been over 70 years in its living and two years in its writing! How do you express such an extraordinary life, not only with its ups and downs but with its uniqueness? Madeleine has the gift of communication by her connectivity with people and the world - or is it two worlds?

I first met Madeleine in 1995, when I began my career in the charitable sector, and walked into the Deaf world for the first time. I suddenly realised I was the disadvantaged one, the one who was missing out on what was being said and struggling to comprehend the intricacies of a new language. I was there in a working capacity to help Deaf people but firstly, did they really need my help and secondly, how could I help when we couldn't communicate?

When I interviewed for the RNID Coordinator position in Cambridge Linda Fincham was part of the interview panel. She was a tough character! In some ways, she barely managed to tolerate hearing people without sign but one day she arrived in the office with her friend, Madeleine. During our chat, where

Madeleine brokered the conversation, she turned to Madeleine and said, "You must teach her". I thought she meant teach me Sign Language (BSL) but oh no! - It was to be much, much more!

Madeleine became my first BSL teacher but it wasn't just the language she imparted to me, it was also Deaf culture and history. Did I realise the damage Alexander Graham Bell caused for Deaf people and Sign Language? He influenced the 1880 Milan Conference to expel Sign Language from schools throughout the world in favour of the oral methodology, which in turn initiated Deaf teachers' expulsion from schools and their profession, and drove Sign Language underground.

WOW! What an education she gave me, could I see the discrimination Deaf people face every day of their lives? I was made to open my eyes and to immerse myself in the beauty and power of Sign Language. This has become a shared passion, though none are quite as passionate as Madeleine!

With Madeleine, I had a pass into the Deaf world, making it not quite as scary as it first appeared. I realised there is 'Deaf speak' - a directness from Deaf people unlike that of the compliant hearing world. This can be a trait exhibited by CODAs! I realised Sign is a Deaf person's first language (even for those who came to signing later in life). English is their second language. Thus, they are often not fluent in the English mother tongue, though incredibly those who have some speech still have a regional accent! Across the counties there are different signs for the same words and numbers.

Publisher's Note

Different countries also have their own definitive Sign Language!

There are Deaf jokes which hearing people do not get and hearing jokes, such as puns, which often bypass Deaf people. Idioms in English don't make sense in sign, such as, *"When pigs fly?"* Plus vice versa, how do you put into English a fabulous expressive sign such as the one for *"Couldn't care less!"*

I learned: Deaf people often say, *"Yes,"* when they have no idea what is said. Many professionals view Deaf people as just having a medical disability rather than fully seeing them divided by a culture and language.

I learned: Sign Language is a full and real language, it has a rich linguistic heritage with its own grammar, syntax and humour.

This is the world in which Madeleine grew up and immersed herself in. As a CODA, she inhabited this indigenous territory and it shaped her life.

The late 1990s was an exciting time as the Disability Discrimination Act came into being. Deaf organisations were able to use this to campaign for simple access in the workplace and other areas. It was a time when Deaf people would meet to talk with Welsh campaigners to compare Sign Language preservation with the Welsh language experience. Welsh was banned in 1536 by Henry VIII. Welsh people have fought to preserve their language and culture ever since. They campaigned for dual name places and instructions on road signs; Welsh speaking TV and radio programmes emerged; the language was taught in schools. Dramatic deeds including 'sit ins' took place to demonstrate the need for duality and preservation of this language to be taken seriously by the government. Finally, in 2011 it received the Royal Assent, from Queen Elizabeth II, to become an officially recognised language.

Deaf people can only dream of the same passion and preservation for Sign Language. Various governments have made promises and Deaf Campaigners continue this fight. In the 2020s there seems more of an appetite to make this happen – we'll see!

Madeleine proudly told me of her family. She was a child of Deaf parents, now known as a CODA. I didn't have the pleasure of meeting her mother, Eileen, but I did meet her father, William.

He had an amazing way with people and I felt my inadequacies in signing really didn't matter to him - he just wanted to engage and know me as a person. Madeleine has inherited this same humanitarian spirit!

In 1995, I was part of the charity 'CRUSE Bereavement Support' and at their annual conference Madeleine and I ran a workshop on *'How to Communicate with Bereaved Deaf People'*. As part of the research, we interviewed William Hempstead using video. He clearly stated his opinions on the subject and shared some of his Deaf history too.

For the report, we asked William about his wife's admission to a care home (due to dementia), and this loss in his life and his understanding of anticipatory grief (as Eileen was still alive). In some ways, he didn't want to talk about it very much but responded to Madeleine's questions, expressing his sadness and philosophical approach to the situation. Here is a short extract:

Madeleine: Do you feel sad?

William: No, no not sad. I miss, miss. Ahh sometimes I see something and go Ahh - tell my wife but she's not there - cos I think she's here - it's a problem.

Later ...

Madeleine: Do you think God made life difficult or easy for Mummy because she is ill? What do you think God makes?

William: Oh well difficult to say, God is not in heaven God is everywhere.

Madeleine: Where?

William: Here, everywhere.

During this interview, William proudly showed me his paintings especially one of Newnham River - he signed, *"Here I used to swim. I used to sit on the green and paint it, it took a long time!"* He also showed me the painting of Madeleine (shown in this book) saying, *"My daughter 12 years, now 37 years - very long time ago."*

This book covers a great deal of Deaf issues and communication challenges, it has avoided some major Deaf political commentary as Madeleine felt this is best coming from Deaf people themselves.

My friendship with Madeleine has spanned 30 years, she continues to teach and support me with my signing. Recently this has been for an amateur dramatic musical production of Godspell. (I hope we shall jointly sign for another amateur production of *Sunshine on Leith*!)

When I began a publishing business with my daughter, Abbirose, I knew Madeleine's story (with a vast knowledge and uniqueness as a CODA) **HAD** to be written and shared with many more people. It is a delight we were able to persuade her, to delve into her memories. One of biggest surprises, and delights, was during her research she gained access to other CODAs with similar experiences in their lives. Her story will continue as she redefines her place in life and comfortably continues to span both Deaf and hearing worlds.

In some ways the reader might need to read between the lines as to what life as a CODA was like for Madeleine and her siblings. How can one really assess the effect of one's own childhood, including the effect of witnessing their parents' discrimination, on their life and personality? Many of her siblings talked about looks from others and discrimination when out with their parents and the safe environment of the Deaf club. We can appreciate their viewpoints via this book, build it into our own understanding of Deafness and make this world a much better place just from reading *We Are CODA*.

Ladey Adey

Publisher and Author of Unfrozen, Ara: A Monkey Puzzle Tree Tale and Successful Business Networking Online

Prologue
CODA: The Film

In 2021, Apple TV+ brought out a film *CODA* (Child of Deaf Adults). The film was honoured with an unprecedented number of awards, including the Special Jury Award for Ensemble Cast, the Directing Award, the Audience Award and the Grand Jury Prize at the Sundance Film Festival in 2021. It also won three Oscar Awards for Best Picture, Best Supporting Actor (Troy Kotsur) and Best Adapted Screenplay for Sian Heder.

The film is a coming-of-age, comedy-drama, where Ruby, an American CODA, attempts to help her family's struggling fishing business whilst pursuing her aspirations to become a singer. British actress, Emilia Jones played the part of Ruby. The actors who played her parents and her brother were Deaf.

Marlee Matlin played the part of Jackie Rossi, (Ruby's Deaf Mother), she is the first really well-known Deaf American Actress. Matlin received an Oscar in 1986 for her role in the film *Children of a Lesser God*. It was a brilliant film.

Troy Kotsur was nominated for eight awards for his role in CODA and won seven of them, including the

Oscar and Golden Globe for Best Supporting Actor and he made history as the first Deaf actor to win a BAFTA (again for Best Actor in a Supporting Role).

Daniel Durant was also notable for his major supporting role in CODA, in the role of Leo Rossi. He is well known for portraying Moritz Stiefel in the Broadway Revival of Spring Awakening, for which he won three awards.

The film portrayed a very positive view of Deaf people and gave them the opportunity to play main roles. It also gave viewers, many of whom may have never met a Deaf person, let alone know a Deaf Community and Culture existed! It did provide a glimpse into the Deaf and CODA worlds.

British Deaf Celebrities

There are British Deaf Actors who have been on stage and screen for many years but sadly mainly recognised within the Deaf Community.

David Ellington is Deaf and communicates in British Sign Language (BSL). He has been in films, TV and adverts, and is a very talented Deaf man.

Rose Ayling-Ellis: played the role of Frankie Lewis in EastEnders, which has been on British screens since 1985. Rose joined the cast between 2020-2022. She also competed in *Strictly Come Dancing* as their first Deaf Contestant. She won the 19th season with her dancing partner Giovanni Pernice. Rose is Deaf with speech.

Soundproof (2006) was a TV film for BBC2. It was the first film which had a mix of Deaf and hearing actors. Soundproof won a BAFTA TV Award for Best

Director in 2007. Susan Lynch, who played the role of the Sign Language Interpreter (she was not a qualified interpreter) was nominated for best Female Actor for an RTS Television Award and Joseph Mawle who played the role of a Deaf man, Dean Whittingham, accused of murder, was nominated for Breakthrough Actor.

Joseph Mawle played the role of a Deaf man accused of murder. Joseph is well known for his role as Benjen Stark in *Game of Thrones*. In *Soundproof,* Joseph has a hearing loss after contracting labyrinthitus.

I also found my way into this film. At first, I was to be an 'extra' in a nightclub scene. Two weeks later I received a phone call from the production team, which made me incredibly excited. Within the storyline, the interpreter 'Susan Lynch', had a relationship with the accused, Dean Whittingham. Having an intimate relationship with a client is against 'Interpreting Standards', therefore the accused needed a new interpreter. My new role was to be an 'older interpreter', for Dean. It was a very small part, but it illustrated how Interpreters must be professional and need to adhere to 'Standards of Conduct'. It was also gratifying to be a fluent BSL communicator playing the role making it realistic; maybe I should have received an award!

Considering it was the first film to have both mixed and Deaf actors, and winning a BAFTA award, I thought it would have greater recognition, sadly it didn't. The film was in BSL and English. The main actors were unable to use British Sign Language although Joseph Mawle and Susan Lynch did learn enough signs for the film. It seems it is more normal for American films to get publicity regarding Deaf actors. Is it because they have more opportunities than British Deaf Actors?

Hearing actors who play the part of a Deaf person/ Interpreter for CODA, have to learn the basic signs needed, normally it would take at least five to six years. American hearing actors can learn to change their accent to an English accent and vice versa. Similarly, a Deaf American actor who has a part to play as an English Deaf character would have to learn a whole new language as American (ASL) and British (BSL) are worlds apart. I am still learning ASL!

After seeing parts of the film CODA, I met with one of my sisters to ask her what she thought about the film. She told me she enjoyed the film but felt it did not portray the real life of a 'real CODA': I agreed. She kept saying, *"There wasn't any sound. All they did was sign all the time."* This just does not happen with Deaf people and CODAs. Deaf people are noisy and often make sound when signing. Then she stated when they acted frustrated and angry it was too different and not something she could relate to. But she did say there were a few moments in the film which did relate to some of her childhood and made her feel a bit tearful at times.

I met with some Deaf friends, at the 'Deaf Together' meeting in Margate a few weeks later and asked them what they thought about the film. It surprised me when their feedback was so different! They saw the film from a Deaf point of view and found it positive and funny. They also said it was great that Deaf actors were being recognised and receiving awards. I said I felt the parents and brother were too quiet, I asked one Deaf friend, *"When you get angry at your partner do you shout at her?"* She thought about it and said she does. She can't hear how loud she is and feels sometimes she is too loud. She said she knows this because hearing people turn round with that 'expression' on their faces. We did giggle as I knew exactly what she meant!

I did not mention the British actress, Emilia Jones, who played Ruby Rossi (a CODA) with my Deaf friends as her role was very different. Ruby Rossi was the daughter who wanted to pursue her passion in singing, but felt she could not leave her family as she was their interpreter. This, I felt was such a good story, but they missed out so much that could have made it funnier, more emotional and more 'real'. Emilia is a very talented young actress who had to learn American Sign Language (ASL). A Deaf friend said why do they do stories on Deaf parents with hearing children who either want to sing or play a musical instrument! I had no answer but it does seem to me as though this storyline is overused and contrived.

Some of the reviews I read about the film had focussed on the response from the Deaf Community. As the film was called CODA and about a CODA, I was very disappointed when I couldn't find any reviews written by any real CODAs. It would have meant something to us CODAs if we had been mentioned or asked.

We Are CODA

Introduction

Mummy and Daddy were Deaf without Speech.

This is not just their story, but a story about a family: with wonderful, warm, loving and emotional memories, plus the frustrations, fears and trust issues Deaf people have within the hearing community.

It has taken more time than it should to tell my story, but life is like that! A few times I have told my publisher it would be much easier for me to sign my story rather than type. Through signing I can show more passion, humour and emotion. Maybe after the book is published, I can sign the book chapter by chapter on YouTube!

Why I Have Written This Book

So many people have said to me, *"Hey you should write a book!"* After many years, I thought, *'Yeah, I can write a book!'* Then, *'What if I write a book that no one will read? Maybe I should write a book as if no one will read it'*, which may be nearer to the truth! However, there is a book in all of us, whether it is fiction or non-fiction. Sometimes you just need a trigger to get you writing, to tell your own story.

This book is about my life within the Deaf Community as a hearing child and adult. To this day, even within the CODA community I have never met another family like ours. No other CODA family I know has ten hearing children with Deaf parents. This is a story about many Children of Deaf Adults (CODA), the 'Unknown Community'. We, CODAs have the responsibility of telling the stories of our Deaf parents and carrying on their legacy. Hearing children of Deaf Parents, used to be known as, *"Mother Father Deaf Me"*, the phrase referred to us as being 'Hearing Children of Deaf Parents'. Now, we are known as CODAs (Children of Deaf Adults).

Last Push

The piece of the puzzle which spurred me to take the final step to writing my story was watching the 2021 Film, CODA. In my mind, it missed the opportunity, to show the richness of the Deaf Community and Culture. Despite this I am grateful to the movie as it gave me the all-important trigger to tell you my story as a CODA and provide more of the depth and colour a CODA experiences within the Deaf Community.

One concern I had writing this book was whether I would remember much from years ago. Luckily, I have managed to recall a significant amount. My memories are mostly still there. There are times when we all tell a story which is not always accurate or has been enhanced to make it sound more interesting! There was so much research I needed to do, as trawling through hundreds of photos, old documents, letters and my large collection of bits of written notes I have

Introduction

gathered over the years. Some people are hoarders of cars, dolls etc. I am a keeper of 'bits of paper', which, I call 'bits of history'. These 'bits' are very important to me. Without these 'bits of history' I would not have been able to write this book.

The most difficult part of writing this book has been holding myself back from writing significantly about Deaf related issues, e.g.. Education, British Sign Language, Government promises, closing of Deaf Schools and Deaf Clubs, because I have been involved in all these issues. I had to keep steering myself to my life as a CODA and reflect on these issues from a CODA view point and try to not 'go all political'. There has been a lot of deleting and rewriting to keep myself on track (and my publisher constantly asking me, how is this relevant as a CODA).

I have always felt it is not up to me as a hearing person to make decisions on Deaf issues. Throughout the stories told in this book, I inevitably scratch the surface of issues which are pertinent to the Deaf but I have tried to hold back on politicising them. Dr Paddy Ladd, who is an amazing and very knowledgeable Deaf author has written many books on 'Deaf Issues', and is a core campaigner for 'Deaf Rights'. He also created the term 'Deafhood'. His writing deals with the issues I mention and is informative and genuine.

Hopefully everyone who buys and reads this book will gain some understanding and have a peep into the 'Life of a CODA'. Those who are CODAs, will most likely be able to relate to my story. This is not to say all CODAs lives are the same, they aren't. It must be so different for Deaf parents having one hearing child, or a mix of Deaf and hearing children and for CODAs who have only one Deaf parent (only 5% of CODAs have both parents who are Deaf).

Throughout the book, I will be use uppercase D for 'Deaf'. Nowadays, it is more common to use lowercase 'd' for 'deaf'. Historically, an uppercase 'D' was used by Deaf people who wanted to describe themselves as being part of a strong Deaf Culture and Community. The lowercase 'd' for deaf was used for people who were hard of hearing, had cochlear implants, couldn't sign and were 'lip-readers' or felt more part of the hearing community. All this has changed now and it up to the person themselves. It is nice not to be 'labelled' with a 'D' or a 'd'. However, I will be using 'D' for Deaf, as I was brought up using this.

There are so many who wanted to contribute to this book, it could have ended up as many books. My parents were loved, respected and admired by many Deaf and hearing people.

Writing this book has been emotionally exhausting, but without my siblings support there would not have been a story, they have been very supportive and at times I have had to change little bits to appease some of them.

The feedback from my Deaf friends has been positive. One Deaf friend loved the Deaf Stories and said she could relate to them. Another Deaf friend said he will definitely buy the book when it is published as he said our family is a 'unique family'.

I hope you enjoy learning more about my Deaf parents, my siblings, my extended family, Deaf and hearing and my life as a CODA.

Madeleine Hempstead, 2024

We Are CODA

What's In A Sign Name?

Names hold great significance in our lives, they anchor us in our social and cultural environments. They encapsulate our identities, heritage, and personal histories, often carrying deep familial and cultural connections. Names are the first gifts we receive, shaping how we are perceived and how we perceive ourselves.

A 'sign name' is unique to the Deaf Culture and Community. Sign names are personal and an easy way to identify someone without having to fingerspell the person's full name. There are three types of sign names.

The first type is a descriptive sign name. This is usually connected to something unique about the person or linked to a person's hobby such as knitting or art. If child has curly hair, then a sign name created could be the sign for 'curly'.

The second type is an initialised sign name - this utilises the first letter of a person's name.

The third type is usually linked to a person's profession, for example if a person is a tailor their sign name may be 'tailor' (a person sewing), a chef may have a chef's hat signed. Even after the person retires this type of sign name may still be retained.

Sign names normally start within a Deaf family and are usually chosen by the family. Our Deaf parents created our home sign names. When we were with the Deaf Community, we would sign 'Beard' (for Hempstead) which was our family sign given because of Daddy's beard. Even today when I meet new people in the Deaf Community, I use the family sign to initiate that I am from Deaf parents, then my own sign name.

Sign names can change as Daddy's did. When he was younger, his sign was for 'tailor' as this was his profession. When Daddy's hair and beard started to turn white, he decided to let it grow long. Due to this the Deaf Community's sign name for him was 'Buffalo Bill', which stuck with him until he passed away. Even today in the Deaf Community, many years after he passed away, he is still known as 'Buffalo Bill'. This sign was two moving gun shapes repeated for the two words.

One of my sisters, was given her sign name by the Deaf community. It was created due to the large earrings she used to wear. She still uses this sign. Prior to this she just used an initialised sign or her number in the family order.

All my siblings would have been referred to by their number or an initialised sign whilst growing up. Now Gabrielle, still uses Number one or fingerspells Gabby.

I use my family sign name to be recognised as child of my father, or I would sign 'Buffalo Bill, father me'. Later, when I worked at the Royal School for the Deaf, Derby I was given my own sign name by the school children, which I still use today, and I am very proud of it. My sign name is 'Mad'. I wonder why?!

Cultural Differences in a Sign Name

A friend of mine used to breed snakes, her 'sign name' was the sign for 'snake'. Her and her partner visited the Deaf Club in Sydney, Australia, where she met up with a group of local Deaf people. At home, in Cambridge she would always introduce herself by her sign 'snake'.

As she introduced herself at the Sydney Deaf Club, with her snake sign name, the room went quiet. Some people giggled and others looked a bit shocked, now she was worried, thinking what have I signed? A Deaf person took her aside and asked where she had got her sign name, she explained she bred snakes. The person was very relieved and explained that the sign name, 'snake' meant something very different in Auslan (Australian Sign Language). It actually meant 'woman who opens her legs!' My friend could not stop laughing, for the rest of her trip she fingerspelled her name, which luckily was short!

Our Family Names

My mother, Eileen, never knew, that as a child, her nickname from her father was 'Chuck'. Auntie Maureen, Mummy's youngest sister remembers it well. She recalls their father would come home after work and ask, "Where is Chuck?" He also carried a photo of Mummy in her pram when he was in the Army and a prisoner in the First World War. I always feel sad that Mummy never knew her own nickname. We don't know why her father called her Chuck. I often wonder what the sign name for Chuck would have been. Would it have made much of a difference to Mummy if she had known? I feel maybe it would.

Mummy went to a Deaf School, where signing was not allowed, she most likely would not have had a sign name or initialised name from her school friends. As far as I know my mother's Sign name was, 'Hempstead Wife'.

We didn't ask our grandmother (Mum) why she chose Eileen as Mummy's name, but we guess it must be connected to the Irish side of our family. Now looking back, I wish I had asked.

Modern Names

Today, society seems to reflect family connections less in the naming of children, it appears to me they are chosen randomly or for entirely different reasons. I have noticed an increase in the popularity of celebrity names and unusual names. One of my granddaughter's is named Etta, after the singer Etta James. This was chosen because her parents liked her music and the name was not commonly heard.

My other grandchildren's names, Isabella, Luella, Theodore and Tilda have all been chosen as their parents liked the names.

My Children's Names

In 1970, while I was training to be a nurse at Cromer Hospital, Norfolk, I met a patient, who was an author, called Sebastian. I thought, 'What a lovely name!' I decided if I ever had a boy, I would choose this name for him. In 1973, my son was born, and I did name him

Sebastian, no family connection at all! The origin of my daughter's name is a whole different story!

All my brothers and sisters have had either all boys or all girls, so I assumed as my first baby was a boy, my second baby would also be a boy. I had chosen the name Claudius (after my grandfather and brother).

In 1977, as I was pushing in the labour ward, I hear, *"It's a girl!"* I told the doctor and nurses, *"It is not possible, it must be a boy; I have a name ready."* I was unprepared for a girl.

A Name! I had to think of a girl's name! I chose 'Emmanuelle'. After the film Emmanuelle, released in 1974. It was the first French X-rated film released by Columbia Pictures. I just loved the name; my daughter's first birth certificate had her as Emmanuelle. After a short time on thinking about her name, I decided it would be best to change her name to Dominique (still no family connection), but it would be easier for my parents to understand. At least I kept a familial French connection!

My Name

I was given the name Madeleine after my great Aunt Madeleine. I learnt it through my hearing siblings and other hearing relatives who said and signed my name, Madeleine. It was easy for me to learn, but no one told me my surname was Hempstead. I started school only knowing my first name.

I remember this fact very clearly because of my first day at school. I was not yet five years old and was sitting in the classroom with our teacher calling out Madeleine Hempstead. I sat quietly, unknowing my surname was Hempstead or what I was supposed to do. The teacher walked up to me and smacked me for not saying, *"Yes Miss"*. I was shocked and started stuttering, *"Yes Miss"*. I had never been smacked before and could not understand what was going on. Even today, if I feel nervous or unsure of how to say words I still stutter. Just writing about this has bought back feelings of sadness and being scared. Naturally, I didn't say anything about this to my parents, it was rare then for a child to go home and tell their parents a teacher had smacked them. At the time, I would probably have been unable to sign fluently to Mummy about the incident!

When I left school and started work, I needed to set up a National Insurance number, therefore I needed my birth certificate. When Mummy gave me my birth certificate, I was shocked. My name was spelled Madeleine! I could not believe it, up until then I had always spelled it 'Madeline'. Even my parents spelled my name without the extra 'e'. The spelling 'Madeleine', after my great Aunt is the French way of spelling it. My parents and best friend spelled my name Madeline for the rest of their lives, even some of my siblings still spell it this way!

Like me, other siblings were surprised when reading their official documentation the first time. Most of my siblings and I are very particular on how our names are spelled and pronounced, it is very important to us. We had grown up ensuring we spoke clearly as possible and pronounced our names precisely.

When it came to our Deaf Community, I was normally asked, *"What number are you?"* I am Number Seven. The Deaf Community knew the children in our family by the number in which we were born. When Deaf people ask me to spell my name, I always tell them it is a long name, most of them lose interest when I say this.

Roman Catholic Influence

My parents were Roman Catholic therefore all ten children were christened as Roman Catholic. I always thought we had three names chosen for us was due to being from a mixed French and Irish from Mummy's parents. However, I was curious to find out more…

I came across a website *www.behindthename.com* and it confirmed to me the Irish link was the reason we had so many names. The website also provided rules to follow in naming children, some of which I talk about, but my parents didn't follow these rules exactly.

The website states, *'The first son is named after the father's father name.'* My eldest brother would have been William John, but he was named Shaun (which is an Irish variant of John).

Then it states, *'The first daughter is named after the father's mother name'*. Daddy's mother was Annetta. My eldest sister is named Gabrielle, but her second name is Annetta. The next two children should be named *'after the mother's parents'* names. If my parents had followed this system their third child would have been called Claudius, but this is not the case.

My second eldest sister would have been named Ethel (which I'm sure she would have changed in a heartbeat) I got Ethel as one of my middle names instead.

The instruction continues, *'The next two children named after yourself and then your favourite sibling or one who died or became a nun or emigrated.'*

Again, my parents did not follow this pattern. Their fifth child should have been named Eileen after Mummy, but this did not happen.

One sibling is named after a character in the film, *The Song of Bernadette*. The film is based on a true story about a young, Catholic, French girl bought up near Lourdes in France. At the age of fourteen, Bernadette Soubirous experienced numerous religious visions of the Virgin Mary. Mummy enjoyed this film very much.

I am Number seven, Madeleine, after a Great Aunt. Number eight is Julian, nobody knows how this name was chosen. Number nine is Claudius, named after our French grandfather. Last of all is Number ten, Francesca, this name was after a girl Mummy and Daddy fostered for about ten years but long before my sister was born.

It is confusing. It took me ages to sort it out!

I wonder why the Irish culture says a child needs three names! We all also use an extra name, chosen for our confirmation, which is from a list of Saint's names.

Between the ten of us we have forty names. Naming a child is difficult for any parent, but you can imagine the increased difficulty for Deaf parents. My parents would have found if extremely difficult as they had to choose three names for each of us, names they could not pronounce or spell! Maybe they put names in a hat and picked them out?! My siblings and I think the Registrar helped to spell most names. Daddy registered our names and he would have had the names written down on a piece of paper.

As our parents could not correctly pronounce our names, they got our attention by using sounds. They often strongly enunciated the initial sound of our names. For example, I might be, *"Ma, Ma, Ma,"*. The sounds were not always clear but using our 'family signs and sounds' we understood who was being called. We had our own form of communication at home. It could be noisy with us shouting to get the attention of a sibling or responding to a call. We also switched lights on and off to get attention. Siblings came in handy if I forgot to tell Mummy or Daddy I was going to the toilet. I would hear them calling for me and have to open the toilet door and shout to a sibling, *"Tell them I am on the toilet!"* Needing to know where people are is a habit I continued with my children, I always asked, *"Where are you going?"* I do it with my grandchildren, too.

When Daddy had a customer to who came to see him for tailoring. It was up to one of us to open the door. When I opened the door with a sunken feeling, I knew I had the responsibility to 'find Daddy'. If he was sitting in his chair in the living room reading the newspaper and I had to tap his shoulder to sign 'man' and point, I knew I would get the look! He hated being interrupted while reading his newspaper. If he was at the bottom of the garden, we would throw something (a small ball or something else small, hoping to get his attention and praying it would not hit him. We were too lazy to

We Are CODA

walk down to get him. Once we had his attention we would sign, *"Door, man,"* and he would know it was a customer and come in. When they could, my brothers left this responsibility to us girls!

When my first child Sebastian was born, I fingerspelled his name and wrote it down to my parents, they never were able to say his name. My second child Dominique was too difficult for them. Mummy asked me, *"Why couldn't you think of an easier name?"* Yes, I was told off!

At her original name, Emmanuelle, my parents would have signed, *"I give up"*. Mummy was unable to lip-read so following the lip-reading pattern would have been impossible. Daddy was better at lip-reading and did make some sounds. We fingerspelled the beginning of our children's names but never shortened them. I would never have signed Seb or Dom. For Sebastian, I fingerspelled 'S' and just one 'D' for Dominique. Daddy would sometimes, give a 'Seb' sound when referring to him or when they played chess. He would just sign, *"Your daughter"* for Dominique.

My
CODA
Siblings

We Are CODA

The Sisters on the Sister's Holiday, Whitstable 2010
Left to Right: Bernadette, Gabrielle, Francesca, Eileen, Josette and Madeleine.

My Five Sisters

I have always felt blessed with my five wonderful, gorgeous sisters. Over the years, many people have asked me, *"Do you get along?"*, *"Do you set one sister against another?"*, *"Do you enjoy spending time with each other?"* and so it goes on.

It is very rare for anyone to say, *"Wow, it must be fun having five sisters!"*, *"It must be great going away together."* Or *"It must have been fun growing up."* Most people seem to assume having five sisters is more of a negative than a positive!

Deaf people normally say, *"How difficult it must have been for your Deaf parents, having six hearing daughters."* Then they ask, *"Do you all sign?"* I answer, "Yes." They often say, "We don't believe you." But after meeting my sisters and I, they say, "How lovely."

We are like any normal bunch of sisters; we have our ups and downs, but all six of us have a very strong bond and involvement within the Deaf Community, Deaf Culture, and the ability to communicate with each other in BSL. This comes naturally to us as we grew up using BSL as our first language. Even today, when my sisters and I are together we use Sign Language.

Occasionally we get the odd look, but we are used to it. During Sign Language week in 2024, we had our annual sisters' holiday and signed every day.

In 2005 my sisters and I are first started the 'sisters' annual holiday', two of my brothers asked, *"Can we come?"* When we said, *"No, just us girls."* They were pretty deflated as they knew we would have fun. Just the thought of all of us spending a week together would either be great fun - pure heaven or pretty hellish.

When I said, *"Hey sisters, I have been 'persuaded' to write a book about our amazing family, what do you think?"* I further explained it was a book primarily about myself with a short section about them as CODAs.

The response from my sisters was mixed but, on the whole, very positive. They were concerned about what

Sisters on Holiday, Harrogate 2013

I would write about them. They said, *"What a task, you must be crazy."*

When I told them, *"Don't worry you can write your own stories,"* they were excited and wanted to know more! There was one request, *"Remember what happens on the annual sisters' holiday, stays on our holiday!"*

This whole book idea was exciting for my extended family (including our 'adopted' Deaf family) and hearing friends who remembered our parents. I felt surprised and emotional that so many wanted to contribute sharing their stories with me. Here I thought it was only going to be me and my siblings.

We Are CODA

Left to Right: Julian, Nickolas, Claudius and Shaun

My Four Brothers

What can I say! I have four lovely, handsome brothers, who loved Mummy and Daddy very much. When all my brothers were at home, especially the two older boys, they were very protective with Mummy. Their communication was limited to 'basic signs' or gestures. They were strong in their 'receptive skills', but weak in their 'productive' ones.

To be able to communicate efficiently, in Sign Language, one needs to have both set of skills for the conversation to be fluent.

Receptive skills in Sign Language means being able to understand what is being delivered, such as gestures and signs, including being able to read body language, facial expressions, including eye gaze.

Productive skills is being able to deliver signs and gestures, including facial expressions, being able be have an equal level in all communication. This means questions, answers, stories, humour and instructions.

Maybe my brothers, made up for their lack of productive skills by playing games, making Mummy laugh and teasing her. Mummy did enjoy all their attention, she knew they loved her but were not able to communicate with her as productively as her daughters could.

During the summer, Daddy would normally make a canvas swimming pool in the back garden. Poor Mummy never stood a chance when the pool was built. She would be in the kitchen, or doing the ironing, washing, cooking or cleaning not knowing when her sons would swoop her up and throw her in the pool, fully dressed. She never heard them coming and she was never prepared. She loved it really, well we hoped she did!

Shaun, the eldest son, was about nineteen, when he decided to join the Army. I can remember seeing Mummy's face and knowing she would miss him very much. Three years later, Nickolas went to join the army as well, the house became much quieter. When my two younger brothers, Julian and Claudius became teenagers, they enjoyed playing games with Mummy. She never got tired of it, and they never got tired of doing it. It is difficult to put in writing about what the games they played on Mummy as they were visual. Our Deaf humour, at home was always visual, we didn't tell jokes we signed them. Some hearing people might say, how could you do that to your mother (put tea towels in her tights while she was washing up? Mummy just kept on washing up).

Gabrielle

There is a lot I can say about my sister Gabrielle, she is the first daughter and the first of ten children. An amazing and wonderful sister loved by us all. I asked Gabrielle if she could send me her memories of when she was a young girl, born during the second world war and being the first of ten children.

Gabrielle is the one who has most of the old photos (which are used in this book), of our parents, Cambridge Deaf Club and Deaf people who we grew up with. She has a beautiful photo of our parents wedding. She also has many photos of Mummy when she was a child and growing up with her sisters. It is different with Daddy, there was only one or two photos of him as a child.

Later on there are quite a few photos taken with him and his awards and achievements, mostly chess and swimming, or dressed as Father Christmas.

Gabrielle's Memories

I was born at our grandparent's house, (Mummy's parents) in Cambridge. Shaun was also born here. It was a very big posh house, my aunts and uncles also lived there. Daddy came to live here after his mother had died (as he could not live with his father), so he moved in with my grandparents and the family.

I was a year old when the Second World War began (September 1939) In the same month and year, Daddy went to Sweden and competed in the Deaf Olympics!

Daddy worked for the Co-op and his wages were £2.00 per week, which was the same as a woman's wage, due to the War. Daddy was excluded from recruitment into the War Effort as he was Deaf.

At that time, all the tailors who worked for the Co-op had gone to War, apart from Daddy. I thought this was quite cruel. Daddy had little work and I believe he felt he could not provide for his family or had any use towards the War effort. He did not feel like a valued man, being rejected must have been upsetting for him.

When I was little but old enough to remember, Mum (my grandmother) and Daddy had a big row, he walked out and left Mummy and us two children with Mum. Daddy went to live with his grandma. As my aunts called my grandmother 'Mum', and grandfather 'Dad', I did as well and from then on all my siblings called then 'Mum and Dad'. We knew our parents were 'Mummy and Daddy', as we normally 'patted' them when we wanted them, but would call them Mummy and Daddy when we talked about them.

My earliest memory was Mummy going to see Daddy at work and she was crying, asking him to come home, but he wouldn't unless Mummy left Mum's house. Shaun was in the pram, and I was sitting on the counter looking at Mummy then to Daddy watching them sign frantically, I remember it very clearly.

Daddy won, we moved to a small house behind a boot shop, in Cambridge and slept in an Anderson Shelter. We would sleep with Mummy and Daddy on the top bunk and Shaun and I underneath. When I heard the air-raid siren (they made a long and very loud warning sound) I would tap Mummy and Daddy and point up, they would then come down where Shaun and I were sleeping and cuddle up with us, I loved it! The lady who lived in a flat above us offered to let Mummy and Daddy know when the siren sounded. They both declined as I would tap them to let them know. *(Author's note: In 1939, The British Deaf Times placed an article of a plan to let Deaf people know when a night-time air raid was taking place. The idea was to connect an apparatus to the Deaf person's bed to the electric circuit of the doorbell. Air raid wardens could then ring the doorbell and the Deaf person would be woken by an electric shock.)*

As I grew older I realised my parents could not hear and their letter writing didn't always make sense as the way they wrote was the same way as they signed! I would go through their letters and correct them.

We used to go to Mum's house for lunch every day as Daddy didn't earn a lot of money. I never remember any awkwardness with communication. My aunts would use basic signs with gestures and so did I. Due to Shaun still be very young, I would sign for Shaun and then for my brother Nickolas. By this time we had moved to a three bedroom, semi-detached council house in Cambridge, where one of my brothers still lives with his family.

We Are CODA

Electric Shock to Warn of Air Raid Siren - Lucky Mummy had a CODA

Gabrielle

The midwife, Nurse Dorrington, attended the births of Nickolas and Josette. I helped her communicate with Mummy. She would always arrive in her smart nurses' uniform, on an old black bike, she would tell Daddy off, *"No more children, not good for your wife!"* Obviously, he didn't take any notice!

When the next sibling was born, the National Health Service (NHS) had been set up, which meant Daddy didn't have to pay for a midwife to attend any future births (not knowing at that time there would be five more births!). Sadly, we never saw Nurse Dorrington again, I guess she was a private nurse.

By then, Daddy had started his own tailoring business in the small third bedroom upstairs, which meant four of us in one bedroom and the baby slept in the cot in our parents' bedroom. The dining room, which was at the front of the house was used for lodgings by an Irish couple. I would love going in there and chatting to them, (or at them!) as I couldn't talk to Mummy or Daddy. As a child, this could be frustrating at times. I am sure I would pick up the Irish accent which would confuse my brothers and sister!

After the Second World War had ended, there was a big party in the street. My dress was muslin and Daddy had painted the 'Union Jack' Flag on the front of the dress. Shaun was dressed in red, white and blue. My husband, David, who lived around the corner, remembers Daddy from this party.

When Daddy moved his 'workroom' downstairs into the front room, the former dining room, his customers would knock on the window to get his attention.

29

If Daddy was sewing, he could not see the customers knocking on the window, then they would start waving. If that didn't work, they knocked on the door hoping one of us, children were home. We were official receptionists!

Mummy and Daddy always made all our friends welcome to the house, even when there wasn't much food, our friends were always offered a sandwich and a slice of cake, if they were lucky! We would play games like musical chairs, hunt the thimble and pass the parcel.

I loved going to the Deaf Club Christmas parties. We would always have so much fun, running around, through adults while they were signing. The Deaf Club was the place where we could be as noisy as want, there was no one signing us to, *"Shhh!"*

My Auntie Yvonne lived with Uncle Stanley; they had two boys, Paul and Stewart, younger than me. Auntie Yvonne paid for my education and I attended St. Mary's Convent in Bateman Street, Cambridge, a fee paying school. All my aunts on my mother's side went there. Mummy attended a Deaf Boarding School. My niece Dominique, Madeleine's daughter, and one of my great nieces, also attended the school. Which means four generations have now attended the school.

Every year the school had a 'Speech Day' at the Guildhall, in town, and I would plead for Mummy to come. One year, Mummy did come and I looked around for her, very excited. I saw her at the back of the hall; she was sound asleep. What an amazing lady!

We lived an isolated life, in many ways, as Mummy's immediate family left Cambridge and moved to London.

Gabrielle

We had gone to Mum's every day for lunch. After they left I went to Auntie Yvonne's as she had decided to stay (she left when I was about thirteen). We were never told the family were planning to leave or why - it just happened! Over the years, we were all sent to stay with various relatives who lived by the seaside in Cromer, North Norfolk.

A Deaf Club Christmas Party, with Madeleine in white at the front.

I spent a lot of time with Mummy and her friends when my children were older or we could ask one my siblings to babysit. Mummy, Irene Hunt, Linda Fincham and I (I was the only hearing one of the group) would go to St. Paul's Catholic Club on a Saturday, where we would drink, laugh and dance the night away, well until about 10.00pm. They were great times. As I was always signing, people thought I was Deaf as well, instead of always trying to explain, I would just smile.

I met my husband David, when Madeleine was a baby, at a Recreational Park in Coleridge Road, Cambridge, he offered me a lift home on the bar of his bike. When he dropped me off at home, he said, *"I remember your dad, he is Deaf."* and that was it! At nineteen, I left home to marry David, before my youngest sister, Francesca, was born. Poor Francesca; she was an aunt the minute she was born.

When I had my children I remembered Mummy's incredible patience, With my four boys, it was the noise and their fights which got to me.

When my husband and I left Cambridge and moved to Liverpool, I missed Mummy very much and the Deaf Community, but I did meet some new Deaf people, but their signing was different, this is just the same for hearing people - we call it a regional accent. The accent of voice is similar to the accent on signing, different words, signs and lip-patterns. I did get confused at times, my 'I am very confused' facial expression was used continually!

Coming back to the Cambridge area made me feel more at home when it came to the Deaf Community.

Gabrielle

Today, my husband and I live in Huntingdon. I go to the Deaf Church and have joined in with the Deaf Community, it feels comfortable as I have known some of them since I was a young girl. Of course, a lot of them have now passed away, which has made me feel I have lost a huge part of my Deaf Life. When Madeleine told me she was writing a book about our Deaf parents and our Deaf Life as a CODA, I was very happy as I feel we are a very 'unique family'. No one has ever heard of Deaf Parents who had ten hearing children, of which I am very proud to be the first.

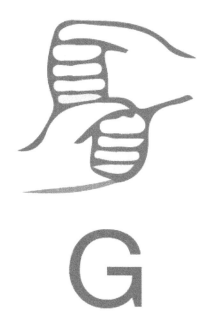

G

We Are CODA

S

Shaun

Shaun is the second child and first boy of ten hearing children.

Madeleine's Memories of Shaun

Shaun joined the army when I was about seven years old. I missed him as he was a very supportive brother.

I have a very specific memory of Shaun telling me off when he was home on leave. I was a rebellious fourteen year old who had gone out and returned home drunk! I thought it didn't matter as Mummy and Daddy wouldn't be able to hear me anyway. I had not realised Shaun was home. When I opened the door, there he stood with Mummy behind him! He was very protective of Mummy and was extremely angry at me for upsetting her. I made sure I never got caught again!

Shaun continues to be a very loving and supportive brother and uncle.

We Are CODA

Nickolas

Nickolas (Nicky for short when we were young) is the third child in the family and the second boy.

Nickolas' memories

Madeleine asked me, what did I feel about having Deaf parents? I first noticed something different when I went round to my friends' houses. My friends with hearing parents could just call out, *"Mum (or Dad) I'm home."* With Deaf parents, I had to find them first, then get their attention by touching them on the arm. What I loved most was that when I signed with Mum, I had her complete attention, she looked at me and only me. At my friends' houses, there was a lot of noise, but nothing as noisy as our house! When you have Deaf parents, you must shout to get your brothers' and sisters' attention. There were seven of us at home then. No one would ever say, *"Keep quiet!"* Well, except for our neighbours!

I felt it was not a problem for Deaf parents to have hearing children but sometimes I felt it was a problem for us. I loved the social gatherings when I was younger, but as I became a teenager I started to hang out with 'bikers' (teenagers with motor bikes and leather jackets).

My 'biker friends' would love coming to our house. I always thought it was a lovely sight with a line of motorbikes outside our home (though it did not go down well with the neighbours!). Whenever they came into the house, they would give my mother a hug and a smile. They loved her. My mother never 'judged them by their looks', they were respectful and loved her fried egg sandwiches and they always had a cup of tea. I taught my friends how to sign, *Please and thanks*. Some of my friends still came round to see Mum after I joined the Army.

Receiving my first pay slip from the Army was great and I decided to send money to Mum. I would write a note and send it with a one pound note, saying the pound was for Mum to help towards food etc. I sent £1 per week for five years. But, as English was Mum's second language there was a 'bit of a confusion!

I became engaged to Sue at the age of 21. Mum gave me money in one-pound notes. I realised this was the money I had been sending to her. I signed, *"For you, help food."* Mum signed back, *"No, you, I saved it for you."* She had thought I'd sent the money for her to save for me!

She refused to keep it and I used it towards my wedding suit which I had handmade from Hepworth, Cambridge! This money story is one of my fondest memories of being a CODA.

Josette

Josette is the second sister and the fourth child. She was named after one of Mummy's sisters.

In our family WhatsApp group, most of us just write a few words and or send a few pictures on a daily basis. Josette makes us giggle as we look forward to her daily comments. You see Josette doesn't just write a few lines, sometimes she writes hundreds of lines. Whatever she writes is always interesting and she always has a lot to say. So, when I mentioned about writing about being a CODA and making it a book, Josette said, *"Really! What is there to say and what do you want from me?"*

Josette uses the word 'profoundly Deaf'. The word 'profoundly' is not used within the Deaf Community, as it is more of a 'hearing word'.

Josette and I are similar, we both have a lot to say. From Josette I have about forty A4 pages of memories, some from the 'recordings', and more from our emails. She also gave me some family photos to use.

Josette is involved in the CDA's History Society. She is helping by sorting through old photos and documents,

Josette's Memories

I was the fourth child: I had a sister who was eight years and two brothers, one who was six years old and one who was eighteen months older than me. My oldest sibling would talk and read to us - signing was a way of life. I didn't know any different.

When I was about seven, my mother took us to the local paddling pool. On the way there we passed by a brook, I signed to Mummy, *"The water is noisy, the stones are rubbing against each other, the water is running fast. Can you hear it?"* Mummy nodded. It was only years later, when thinking about this time, I realised she could not hear it but she didn't want me to get upset. Around the same time my father sat me and two other siblings down and taught us to sign the alphabet and some numbers, 1-10, 20, 30 and so on up to 100 and 1,000.

After me, Mummy had six more children, and it was not until she was pregnant with the youngest sibling, I was aware of her being pregnant. I would have been about thirteen years old.

Life to me was normal, we were very noisy as we were never told to be quiet I was used to it. Both my children are noisy as well. As a child I loved the library, it was my haven. I could go home with a book, curl up and block out all the noise going on around me.

As a family we were taken to the local Deaf club, where we played with other children, Deaf or hearing, there was no trouble as we all signed. When we were older, we were able to go to the cinema to see a film. My mother love films, as long as they were action without too much talking. I still enjoy a good film. As I got older, I would be one of the siblings to listen to what the people in our area said about what was going on at the schools and in general gossip, and then relay it back to Mummy.

On firework night, we had fireworks and a huge bonfire. We made a Guy Fawkes by collecting leaves, Daddy helped us by getting some old clothes, then we would sit the guy on top. We had jacket potatoes, which were put into the bonfire, with butter. Christmas Day and our birthdays were always special days; we each had a party to make it special to us.

I remember Daddy telling me he was offered hearing aids when he was at Margate Royal School for the Deaf. He enjoyed being at the school so he refused them. He was worried he would be labelled hearing and be moved. He said he preferred being Deaf. He felt by being Deaf with hearing aids he would not belong to either the hearing world or the Deaf world.

Deaf Club Outings and Games

As far back as I can remember, I would go to the annual Deaf Outing to the seaside. It was fun going on the coach; having fish and chips and ice cream was such a treat.

At the Deaf Club we had brilliant parties and we would all play games. Pass the Parcel was a favourite: the gift was wrapped in newspaper. A man, mostly my father, would stand in the middle wearing a blindfold and holding a handkerchief. He would swing the hanky around his head. When it came down, it was the holder's turn to rip off a sheet from the parcel. The parcel then moved on again until the prize was revealed. Other games we played were Musical Chairs and Musical Statues. When we were older, we played line games, usually alternating with a lady then a man. They were fun.

As an adult, I still went to the Deaf parties and took my children. There was no problem for any of the children as they had their cousins there. They never seemed to have any trouble communicating with the Deaf children.

I took my granddaughter with me to a meeting at the Deaf Club as they were showing a video about my father. Everyone made a fuss of her and asked her name, which she signed for them. She was seven years old.

CODA Interest

A few years ago, a local primary school in Cambridge asked if I would talk to the children about being a CODA. This was during Deaf Awareness Week. They asked the typical questions. I was asked, *"How did you learn to speak?", "How did you learn to sign?", "Did it take a long time to talk to your parents?"* I explained there are signs for most things such as mummy, daddy, brother sister, places, toys and so on. Two hours went by very quickly. The children, and the teachers, learned a lot about what CODA meant.

Josette

Not Different At All

Deafness is thought to be different, but I don't remember it being a problem. I never thought of my parents as being different. All my friends got on with them very well.

Mummy loved *The Birdie Song* by The Tweets and *Oops Upside Your Head* by The Gap Band. We all called it, *The Rowing Song*. Both of these songs had dance moves. Mummy would watch us and soon joined in: we had good times.

J

We Are CODA

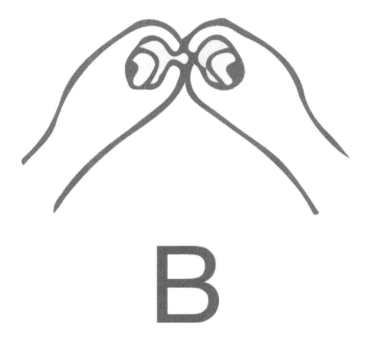

B

Bernadette

Bernadette is the fifth child and the third daughter in the family.

Bernadette's Memories

I was born in Cromer, Norfolk. Mummy had gone to visit her mother and whilst she was there, she received a telegram telling her it was best she stay in Cromer to have the baby as the other children at home had chickenpox.

When I was one year old there were five siblings living in our house. At this point in my life, I clearly had no comprehension of my parents being Deaf. I was just growing up in a large family. It wasn't until I started school I became aware my mother and father were different.

Communication

A large part of our lives was attending the Deaf Club. This was the main part of our social lives until we went to school, there was no nursery school for us.

Daddy was able to communicate with Deaf-blind people, signing letters on their hands. There was one woman, in particular at the Deaf Club, who would have such a chuckle when Daddy was communicating with her. I often wondered what they were talking about.

My parents were very committed to the Deaf Community. Mummy was part of the Mothers' Union and Daddy a member of the CDA Committee. He had been Treasurer, Chair (at different times) and once was part of the British Deaf Association.

They were very popular and as their children, we were very proud. Even to this day, at any occasion with the Deaf, when I sign, *"Hempstead"* older Deaf people remember my parents and smile signing, *"Mother father know well, loved them."*

My children went to the Deaf Club too, particularly the Christmas Parties where they would see their cousins.

My Parents

My father was skilled at so many things. He was a magician performing at the Deaf Club at Children's parties and at Christmas.

It always amazes me, when my parents travelled abroad on holiday and went to a local Deaf club, within half an hour or so they had picked up each other's signs and were able to communicate. This happened in Spain, France, Italy and a few other European countries. They loved going on their holidays in later life.

Going on Deaf Club Outings

The Deaf Club summer outings were amazing and such fun. I can still picture the coach, it would arrive at Great Yarmouth, Clacton-on-Sea or some other East Anglian seaside town and we all piled out, all signing away and laughing. There would be blankets, packed sandwiches in baskets and our bathing suits and towels: we would race off to see who would be the first one in the sea.

The adults 'piled out' of the bus, circa 1950

Daddy was a very strong swimmer, a world champion, and would always be the first in the water. Daddy taught me to swim and by the age of five; I was a pretty good swimmer. When Daddy finished his swim, he would get dressed have a sandwich and then go to the pub to join the other Deaf men. We stayed on the beach with Mummy, waiting for our ice cream after our lunch and spend the rest of the time making sandcastles and playing. The younger ones would have a sleep under a towel to protect them from the sun. The Deaf always knew how to enjoy themselves, there was little complaining. They didn't seem to help each other much but I think it goes back to their school days. All would have attended schools for Deaf children where they were taught to be resilient, self-sufficient and not to rely on others. Some were allowed to sign at school, but most were not, therefore their signing would be basic (they were taught in different ways).

My three girls often went on Deaf Outings with their aunts and cousins sometimes Deaf people would sign, *"Hempstead Outing"* on the coach. They do remember those times of fun and something so different from their other social lives.

Working with Deaf People

Today I am involved with the Bury St Edmunds Deaf and Hard of Hearing Association where I have been a Trustee and Volunteer. When I was in Cambridge, during the 1980s, I was the Community Worker at the Deaf Centre, my role was to represent Deaf people within the Local Authority trying to ensure they had equal opportunities and were represented at all levels. At that time, BSL was not recognised as a language and many Deaf people had difficulties in finding an interpreter for official appointments.

As a CODA, I have always seen myself as part of a 'dual culture'. I am Deaf and hearing and belong to both worlds and I am pleased to say my Deaf Community see me this way too.

Eileen

Eileen is the fourth daughter and the sixth child. It must have been difficult for our mother to cope, as there is only fifteen months age difference between Eileen and me.

The age difference meant I had a close sibling growing up. Over the years, Eileen has been a supportive, caring and loving sister.

E

We Are CODA

Madeleine

I am the seventh child and fifth girl. I was born six years after the Second World War ended when there was still rationing (rationing finished in July 1954). Regularly, I hear older people talking about how tough their upbringing was during the war and the hard times they experienced as a family. This makes me think about the difficult times we had growing up in Cambridge. Like every other family, we were brought up on rationed food and very little money, being Deaf didn't exclude my parents from the rationing and in some ways it may have been even more difficult, but they just got on with life.

Our Language

Our first language at home was Sign Language. I spent many hours watching and learning with my little eyes going to and fro from my parent's hands and facial expressions to my older siblings (a bit like watching a tennis match!). It was sometimes frustrating trying to communicate with my parents while learning how to structure my sign. I wanted to be able to do more than simple gestures.

We Are CODA

A Numbering System

Deaf people outside of the family found signing our names difficult. So, my parents decided to sign the number we came in the family, I was known as 'Number seven', as I was the seventh child. Even today, I am sometimes still known as Number seven. The only one who was not known by a number (Number ten) was my youngest sister, her sign was 'Baby'.

Oil Painting of Madeleine by Daddy

A Noisy World

Living with nine loud, hearing brothers and sisters and Deaf parents, who did not have speech, meant life at home was never boring. At times I felt desperate for some quiet from all the noise (I am sure the neighbours did as well). There was always extra people staying too. Mummy 'fostered' a girl, called Francesca (not my sister) for eight years and we had many of our cousins to stay, especially during summer holidays.

As a teenager I struggled. I went to the local Youth Club on my own at the age of twelve, my parents didn't ask me where I was going or what time I would be back. Having many teenagers at home must have been difficult for my parents.

Hearing parents get frustrated and angry at their teenage children when they fight, slam doors and make noise. Our parents never got angry or frustrated at this, even though we made a lot of noise, as they were simply unaware of the extent of the volume. Our neighbours on the otherhand...

There was no point in shouting, *"I am going out now!"* and slam the front door. I wouldn't even bother to tell a parent I was going out, I just went! There was no point asking my siblings to let my parents know, they always forgot or did not know how to sign well enough. This is an example of the freedom my siblings and I were given, a freedom most teenagers would crave!

The only time I remember Mummy getting angry at me was when I wouldn't stop badgering her for money. She turned sharply and made a guttural growl. Her eyes were wide and wild, her signing frantic. I was so shocked. I apologised immediately. It never happened again.

We were brought up unable to shout for our parents when we returned home. We had to search for them, this was just part of being a CODA. In our family, we knew Mummy would either be in the kitchen, knitting in the sitting room or putting the washing out or bringing it in. We would either wave or tap her and sign, "*Home me.*" I remember I would always have a kiss; Mummy was very loving.

I learnt how to communicate my 'happy' emotions with my Deaf parents, by laughing, joking and using humour, it was easier than trying to sign, "*I feel sad*" or "*Friends are teasing me at school.*" I tucked these feelings away.

Each sibling communicated in their own way. My sisters and I found it easier to communicate using sign with our parents. My brothers used humour, joking and playful teasing and basic gestures as their form of communication. I think this limited how much expression they could put into what they said to them.

We were told very little by our parents about what was going on. I was told by Gabrielle that Mummy had gone to a 'Convalescing Home', in Norfolk, after she had one of the babies. This didn't mean much to me at the time: all I can remember is one of our strict hearing aunts came to look after us.

Relationships Outside of Family

When my best friend, Diane, came over to my house, she just didn't just come over to play with me, she had to play with the others as well. Diane also came to the Christmas Parties, she loved them too. If any of us brought boyfriends or girlfriends home, my siblings would be noisy and nosey and ask questions like, *"Do you like each other? Do you kiss each other?"* We all thought it was funny when it wasn't us being questioned. Most of my brothers-in-law and sisters-in-law are unable to sign but they all tried to communicate with Mummy and Daddy in the best way they could. They were all welcomed and understood.

Moving Out

I moved to London at sixteen; Mummy still had my three younger siblings to think about. There wasn't a phone at home which meant I had to write to my parents from London, just to let them know I was still alive! Communication about what I was doing and where I was not good; in fact, it was basically non-existent! Mummy knew I was with my friend Vivian (she had recently moved to England from Shanghai, China). Vivian was twenty-one, five years older than me, and she wasn't always a good influence! She loved my parents very much and called my mother 'Mum', to the annoyance of one of my sisters.

At times it was frustrating not to have a spoken language, to not to sit there and just have a chat. It was almost impossible, until I was much older, to have the time to sit down and have a one-to-one time with Mummy or Daddy. As a family, we all had 'family attention and time' but not very often as 'one-to-one'. This did mean my relationship with all nine siblings is strong; we

We Are CODA

Madeleine the Rocker at Bury St Edmund's Deaf Club

are close and very supportive of each other all these years on.

My main memories of Mummy growing up are as smiling, patient, laughing, signing and always with food on the table - and of cuddles, kisses and lots of love.

Communication may have been easier with hearing parents. I would have been able to talk about what I was doing and about going to London while my parents were washing up, in the garden or even having a meal! They couldn't sign easily whilst they were doing their tasks.

Sometimes I wonder if my time 'off the rails' in London was an outlet for me to manage my limited home communication and attention from my parents. When I lived in 'swinging sixties' London, I didn't feel emotionally comfortable with hearing people, there was just too many of them. My comfort zone was with Deaf teenagers and with the Deaf Community in Cambridge, where I grew up.

Welcomed into the Deaf Community

Being a hearing child of Deaf parents, my five sisters, four brothers and I have always felt welcomed and accepted in the Deaf Community. I have always considered them to be my extended family. My siblings and I were part of the Deaf Club and Deaf Events.

Deaf Club Games

We played many games at the Deaf Club: The Boy and Girl Orange Game. This game had two even lines, each line had alternating boys and girls. The front boy would have an orange under his chin and a balloon in between his legs and he had to pass it onto the girl making sure he had the orange under her chin and a balloon in between her legs. She then had to turn round and pass it on to the next boy, and so it went on until the first team finished without dropping the orange or the balloon. If anyone touched the orange or balloon with their hands, they had to start all over again.

One of the Many Deaf Games at the Deaf Club
Mummy is in the front centre

My favourite game was Musical Chairs. Men would sit on the chairs and Daddy would be on the stage, with his back to us, swinging the hanky over his head. We had to look at him, to wait for the hanky to drop, which was mayhem in itself! We would walk slowly backwards around the chairs and when the hanky dropped it was a free for all, with so much laughter. We Hempstead girls normally won, the men on the chairs would love it, they weren't allowed to touch us or drag us onto their laps. Everyone was very flirty but

I loved going and having fun, it was so different from the hearing world. I found the hearing world were not always keen on playing these games, as it would not be the 'correct thing to do'.

Identifying the Hempsteads

Members of the Deaf Club had their own way of identifying us, as a family and individually. We, 'The Hempsteads', were well known in the Deaf Community, not just in Cambridge but in Deaf Clubs based in East Anglia: Ipswich, Bury St Edmunds, Norwich, Lowestoft, Great Yarmouth, Peterborough and King's Lynn. Happily, I can report these Deaf Clubs are still open today but the hours have been reduced. Instead of opening every Saturday, they are open either every two weeks or monthly. Many open during the week rather than on Saturdays.

My Grown Up Thoughts

My brothers and sisters and I have chatted and debated about how different our lives would have been if we had been bombarded with missionaries, social workers or even interpreters interrupting our family life - like so many other Deaf families experienced. Even today, we still discuss how fortunate we were.

I wonder if we were selfish? We were happy how our lives were. We didn't think about support our parents needed. We were children: we thought our parents were like all other parents and being Deaf did not mean to us that they were any different! I wonder if Deaf children of hearing parents feel the same! Or, maybe we were protecting our parents and family from outsiders, people who didn't understand our home culture!

Now, as a parent, I feel if we had understood how our parents must have always struggled, we would have wanted them to have more support. It makes me feel sad as it never occurred to me Mummy would have found life very hard bringing up ten hearing children; find it so demanding, so exhausting to find countless ways to communicate with each of us. Mummy did receive some support from her mum and sisters but was it really enough?

Today

In January 2023, I became involved with a group of mixed-age Deaf people to look through archives to prepare and celebrate the last one hundred years of history of the Cambridge Deaf Centre.

We have looked through hundreds of old photos, documents, letters and newspapers clippings ready for the centenary in 2027. I felt comfortable sitting around the table looking through the archives, even as the only hearing person there; it was as though I was looking through old family photos. They are the people I grew up with and their children are the children I played with. It has been difficult for me to cope with the deaths of many of them. A lot of them were friends of my parents, but became more like aunties and uncles to me. We had Deaf Outings with them, they came to visit the house and we had Christmas Parties together (best parties ever).

Madeleine

John Fincham (who is now 80) sat next to me: we were the only two people who had been part of the Deaf Club since we were babies.

A few of the documents, we went through had the surname Hempstead mentioned. Daddy was first mentioned in the Deaf Diocese Log Book in 1930, when he was 18 years old. The Deaf Diocese Book was set up in 1909, to record each Deaf person in the Diocese. Over the years, different people were responsible for keeping the book up to date. One of these people was Mr. Rowland. He always looked old: he was small, with a bent body and wore metal rimmed glasses. His hair was white and he always wore a pinstripe suit, which I think was as old as him! He had the kindest smile, children would run to him at the Deaf Club, and hug him, including my son, Sebastian.

I also remember John Hay, the East Anglian Deaf Historian, at Peterborough Deaf Club when he visited. He showed videos of Deaf meetings, rallies and conventions going back over seventy years. These videos had been copied from old reels which had been found. Some of them were saved from skips when Deaf clubs and schools had closed down. He was trying to put faces, names, dates, and locations together for the British Deaf Association.

It was emotional to see some of the Deaf people at the club help him out with names, places and dates, and to see their faces light up when they recognised an old school friend or a Deaf gathering they attended. Seeing Daddy on video at the Deaf Olympics for the first time was very emotional for me. I put my hand up and signed, *"I know who that is!"*

We never called my parent's friends by their first name, it was seen as rude and disrespectful, we signed their names, we may not know what their surnames were but we knew their sign names. Mr. Germany was sign for Germany, Mr. Swallowe was sign for Swallow (the bird) and Mr Fincham we spelt his name. We didn't know any of their first names, apart from Irene and Arthur Hunt.

Unfortunately, many of these loved people have passed away. Either myself or one of my siblings attend the funerals. I remember attending Daddy's best friend funeral, Mr. Swallowe. Mr. Swallowe went to Margate Deaf school with him. They both went from Cambridge

Mummy with Mr Swallowe

when they were seven; from then they were the best of friends. It was sad to see Daddy so upset. Not only was he burying his best friend, but his wife was ill with dementia and living in a care home.

My Community

Life has always kept me involved with the Deaf Community. I am fully immersed in the Deaf world, even though I am hearing. Many people have mistaken me for being Deaf, which I take as a compliment, but I would like to confirm I have never said I am Deaf.

Even today, my life is still more in the Deaf World than in the hearing. It is a place where my heart feels more comfortable and I am less anxious. It is a culture and community where my passion is and my heart belongs.

We Are CODA

Julian

Julian is the eighth child and third son. I enjoyed asking Julian about being brought up with Deaf parents.

Julian Memories

I was never told our parents were Deaf; I just knew. When I started trying to shout at them or say something, I guess even as a toddler, I knew they couldn't hear me, but my older siblings could! When I was a teenager, I could get away with saying things, they would not have wanted to hear!

I was the first boy after four girls. I remember at times having to fight for survival, to get attention, but I think this is the same in any large family whether parents are hearing or Deaf.

I remember bringing friends home. Sometimes I would tell them my parents were Deaf before I brought them home but I never really saw it as being negative, I just told them to prepare them as they may have difficulty in speaking to them. I never experienced people thinking Mummy and Daddy as foreign or strange, but they did talk funny.

Having Deaf parents was possibly negative in terms of being limited in terms of communication with them, but I can't compare the experience to as if they were hearing. However, I had fun in the Deaf Community, on the Deaf outings and the Deaf Christmas parties. My signing skills were not very good, but I could understand more when Deaf people signed.

I think we all signed clearly enough, otherwise Mummy or Daddy would not understand what we were saying. It wasn't all about signing, there were gestures, pointing, showing or asking another sibling what sign was needed to sign something brief, for example, *"Friend mine go their house?"* with a pleading look on my face. We never had to write anything down.

Deaf people have a very good sense of humour and they like visual humour best. They would laugh at themselves and amongst each other. Maybe it is because it felt safe in a small group. It was never acceptable for hearing people to laugh at them. Daddy got his fists out on a few occasions at the local pub!

I stayed at home until I married Vivien. After we married I would go round to the family house on Fridays and this continued after my daughters, Kellie and Verity, were born.

Claudius

Claudius is the fourth brother and ninth child. Claudius had a lot to say, which is normal for him.

Claudius' Memories

I remember being at home with only four sisters and one brother, Julian, as my older siblings had moved out. I never thought of being brought up in a 'big' family. We went to a Roman Catholic School and a lot of the children were from big families. We were the only family who had ten children, though. We didn't have much money, but it wasn't important, and we did have lovely neighbours. I still live in the house I was born in.

I think we were a bit of a novelty. When I got to secondary school everybody knew who I was and I had barely started. Daddy never came to the school. Mummy came sometimes, but must have been difficult for her without any communication support. I think this is why hearing people don't mix with Deaf people, it is communication thing.

It was awful in some ways, because I could embarrass my friends so easily because Mummy and Daddy were not like anybody else. There was something more intimate in our relationship with Deaf parents, they were very tactile. I noticed a big difference when I visited homes of my friends. I could chat away to their parents however when my friends visited our house they couldn't be chatty and did not say anything. Yet, they loved coming to our house, they called it a 'Happy House'. My friends adored our parents. They thought it was incredible, how we communicated with our parents, brothers and sisters by signing and speaking. I always found it interesting when they said this, as far as I was concerned it was normal. Both Mummy and Daddy had a good sense of humour, it was a must with so many hearing children - it was not easy for them!

In January 2023, I went back to Cambridge Deaf Club, and it was wonderful to be back in the Deaf community again. They were changing the name of Cambridge Deaf Club, known as Hope Hall, to Fincham House after Linda Fincham, who was a previous committee member who dedicated a lot of time to the CDA.

Fincham House where we attended many parties and events and some of us still do!

Claudius

We all grew up with the Fincham's at our house and I remember Linda so well, she was like a Deaf sister, I liked her. I was sad to hear she died of cancer in 2018.

Claudius and Daddy

C

We Are CODA

F

Francesca

Francesca is the youngest; the tenth child and the sixth sister. By the time Francesca was born, Mummy was 43 years old which in those days was very old to have a baby. Now, many mothers are having their first baby in their forties or even fifties!

Due to Mummy's age, Francesca was born in Mill Road Maternity Hospital. Even to this day, I remember Daddy coming home after he had seen her, he had a big smile on his face and signed, *"Peach baby."* In BSL signing 'Peach' means the skin was very soft. I still call her the 'Peach baby'. Francesca always replies, *"Daddy looked at the wrong baby!"* Or maybe Daddy meant, 'Breach not peach baby!'

Francesca's Memories

By the time I was born, there were only two brothers and four sisters still at home. This meant during school time I was the only child at home, as the rest were at school or working. When my sisters and brother got home they didn't automatically start chatting away to their baby sister, they just signed away.

Fresh Cream Cakes

Mummy knew Madeleine and I loved fresh cream cakes (it had to be fresh cream!) as much as she did!

Mummy would buy either fresh cream slices or chocolate éclairs on a Friday afternoon. These fresh cream cakes would be put in the fridge until Mummy had time to sit down with a cup of tea. Well, of course this was far later than Madeleine and I would like, we always felt we could give Mummy a 'helping hand' to eat the cakes.

I would look in the fridge and just see them sitting there waiting to be eaten. Sometimes, I would tap Mummy on her shoulder and feeling very smug, sign to her, *"Madeleine put her finger in cake in fridge!"*

Of course, Madeleine would sign, *"Never me, Francesca lie."* However, Mummy would give Madeleine her, 'you naughty girl' look. I would be giggling behind Mummy, as I would try anything to get those cream cakes out so we could eat them.

On one occasion, when I tried to get Mummy to tell Madeleine off, Mummy turned to look at me with the same, 'you naughty girl' look. I had been caught!

Many times Mummy would allow Madeleine and I to share her cream cakes, which we did with passion and smiles... and we all ended up with cream on our faces, especially Mummy. Even today, Madeleine and I love fresh cream cakes and have fond memories of our cake sharing Fridays.

Francesca

White Exhibition

As an adult I can remember visiting the 'White Exhibition' at The Whitechapel Gallery in London with Madeleine. I thought it was a 'Silent Exhibition' as it was so quiet! We walked into one of the exhibition rooms, which was painted white, with a white painting on the wall. Thank goodness we didn't have to wear white! We sat down quietly on the bench, which was in the middle of the room and started signing to each other, which is pretty normal for our family.

People came into the room and whispered to each other, *"Oh! I think these two women signing must be part of the exhibition."* Madeleine and I looked at each other and signed, *"Let's get out of here!"* We giggled about this and still do. I wonder why they thought we were part of the exhibition. If we were talking, would they have thought the same?

Madeleine's Additional Reflections

I think Mummy wanted Francesca to benefit from attending a local nursery to mix with hearing children. When she went to look at the nursery; the staff could not communicate with her. They then sent Mummy a letter stating they could not offer her daughter a place! They never told her the reason. I guess this is why Mummy took Francesca everywhere with her while the rest of us were out.

Mummy spent a lot of time with her and loved taking her (and all of us) to the cinema. Maybe going to the pictures was Mummy's way of giving us access to the voices of hearing people.

We Are CODA

Left to right: Eileen, Francesca, Bernadette, Madeleine, Gabrielle, Josette, Julian, Claudius, Nickolas and Shaun (2017)

Back (left to right): Gabrielle, Shaun. Nickolas, Josette and Bernadette
Middle: Eileen, Madeleine, Julian, Claudius and Francesca
Front: Daddy and Mummy (early 1980s)

My
Deaf
Parents

We Are CODA

*Auntie Maureen, Auntie Josette, Mummy, Mum, Auntie Pauline
(Behind) Auntie Yvonne*

Mummy
Eileen Sibellas
1916 - 1998

Mummy was born in 1916, at the Army Barracks in East Blatchington, Seaford, near Portsmouth, and given the name Eileen. She was the first child of Claudius and Ethel Sibellas. She had four sisters, Josette, Yvonne, Pauline and Maureen.

I'm not quite sure when Mummy lost her hearing. We all have discussed it and think she was about a year old; she had meningitis and spent a long time with ice wrapped in towels at the base of her neck to bring down her temperature down. Eventually she recovered, which was a blessing: it was a real life and death situation. Mummy became a healthy and bubbly little girl but totally lost her hearing. When her parents called her name, she didn't respond, they weren't worried as she had been ill and they thought she was catching up or just being lazy. This has been repeated to me by a lot of Deaf friends. Their hearing parents were all told by 'well-meaning' professionals, *"Your child won't respond to you because they are lazy."* This is one reason many Deaf babies were about three or four years old before they were eventually diagnosed as being Deaf.

After the diagnosis, Mummy's parents were told she must go away to a Deaf Residential School, but they didn't want her to go. In the end, she stayed at her grandmother's house and went to Miss Tailor's private

Mummy (centre) at Miss Tailor's Private School

day school. Later, from the age of ten or eleven, she attended Oak Lodge School for Deaf Girls in Balham, as a boarder, where she stayed until she was sixteen. She was classed then as 'Stone Deaf'. Now they use the term, 'Profoundly Deaf'.

During school time all the girls were forced to use speech, as it was an oral school where signing was banned. They were taught to communicate through lip-reading and use of speech! Sometimes they would hold apples or balloons to their mouths and feel the vibration of sounds. To stop the girls from trying to sign, their hands were tied to the chair. After school the girls were watched to make sure they did not try and sign to each other. In the evenings, and especially at bedtime, the girls had socks tied on their hands, yet again, to stop them from trying to sign. This was how Mummy went to bed. Her hands were rarely free.

Mummy and Daddy both told me when they were at school, Deaf children had a basic education and were trained to do manual work such as sewing (which Mummy did), cooking, cleaning and laundry. Mummy told us about the poor girls who worked in the laundry - one their jobs was to boil sanitary cloth towels. Just the thought of it, yuk!

Mummy was very happy at the school and made lifelong friends (both my parents did). All of her friends were Deaf and many of them became my extended Deaf family. Mummy never really felt comfortable with hearing people, apart from family, she never had a hearing friend.

We Are CODA

Shy Mummy Behind Dad (My Grandfather)

Mummy

I'm not sure when Mummy and her family moved to Cambridge, or what bought them to Cambridge. It may have been my French grandfather (Dad), Claudius' work. He was a chef and worked in various high-class restaurants and been a chef on The Royal Train for Queen Victoria. Or, perhaps they moved out of London due to the First World War. Due to my parents being Deaf, they were not told much about their early life, the history of their families or even their parents' names! I know more about my extended Deaf family than my own relatives.

Mummy first went to the Deaf Club when she was fourteen, she told me she was scared and was hiding behind her father, so shy and shocked, she had never seen anyone signing before and here they were, young and old, using their hands, very quickly, to talk to each other. She remembered they were smiling, confident and caring and welcomed her with open arms. The story within the family says Mummy was so scared it took her three years to go back into the Deaf Club.

When Daddy saw her on her next visit, he really liked her, so did William Fincham, Roy Brown and a few other young Deaf men. Daddy was fluent in Sign Language, and he was very kind. He helped Mummy to sign as she had been restricted from using signing. Though she could not speak she had learned how to write. Later, as she got better at signing, English was her second language.

Mummy and Daddy married in the Roman Catholic Church, in Cambridge on December 27th, 1937, and stayed married until they both passed away.

Wedding Night

In Mummy's time, it was normal for young women only to be told about sex and how babies were born after they were married. Or if they were lucky, just before to warn them what was going to happen!

Mummy was very open with her daughters. She shared her story of her wedding night. She did not know what to expect. She cried. Daddy was very loving, and told her it was part of married life and he loved her. The next day she went to see her Mum who said, *"Yes, it is normal, it's okay!"*

Wow! How difficult it must have been for her to understand what all this meant. When I was having my babies in hospitals, I had midwives, support, doctors talking to me telling me what was happening and a very supportive team. Mummy had little or no communication, or support, her births were supported through facial expressions and gestures and the lovely Nurse Dorrington.

What would have happened if she had ever needed a caesarean? There were no interpreters, no one other than the health professionals were allowed to be in the room with her. Her husband had to stay outside the room.

Having Babies

Mummy was 21 when Gabrielle was born, only ten months after they got married. Little did she know she would be spending the next 22 years being pregnant, giving birth to another nine children! All the births were normal births, eight which were at home, one in North

Norfolk - exact location still unknown to this day, and the youngest was born at the local Maternity Hospital. Unfortunately, Mummy did suffer one miscarriage.

In addition to her own children, she also looked after other children, including a hearing girl called Francesca (not my sister) from the age of six weeks until she was eight years old.

We had a family doctor, Dr Shepherd, who was also a close friend of the family. He was a wonderful, kind man and although he could not sign, he always made time to explain everything clearly to Mummy. I can remember he did a lot of house visits to us; it could have been because his surgery was up a flight of steps by the side of his house and the pram could not get up them.

Daily Routine

Mummy was a hard working, loving and attentive mother. Every morning, we were woken up with a shake of the shoulder, a kiss on the cheek and a lovely hot cup of tea. Before school, at breakfast, after school and at bedtime, we always had a kiss on the cheek from Mummy.

Being bought up with lots of children, did mean I sometimes would have to fight for attention. With a hearing parent, it is normally the child who shouts the loudest who gets the attention. This would never have worked with us. It was the child who was most fluent in Sign Language got the most attention. I have been told by my siblings, that was me!

Sometimes I think Mummy must have been worn out physically, mentally and emotionally as her life every day was looking after the children and to ensure when we went out, we were children to be proud of. Even though I didn't often have one-to-one time with her, due to there always being another sibling around, I always knew I was loved.

Mummy's daily routine was the same for years. I have outlined it here (if it was me, I would not have lasted a year!).

Mummy's Routine

4.30am - up boil nappies, wash clothes, use the mangle to get rid of excess water of the clothes.

5.00am - hang clothes outside regardless of the weather (I remember clothes on the line being as stiff as a board).

5.30am - on her knees washing the lino in the sitting room.

6.00am - feed and dress the baby and any toddler.

7.00am - wake up children who went to work or school with a cup of tea in bed. A sister remembers, "We were all woken up with Mummy. She would come upstairs with a tray into the girls' bedroom (five girls shared the bedroom), tap us on the shoulder to wake us up with a cup of tea."

7.30am - place all our school clothes on the end of the bed and polished shoes and brushed coats by the front door.

8.00am - Look after remaining babies and children while we were at school, prepare meals and complete household chores.

Mummy

11.00am - Mummy and Daddy had their coffee break, Mummy would go into Daddy's workroom, sign 'coffee'. They both sat down together at the table, which Daddy had made, to have their coffee. Even now, most of us have a break at 11.00am, regardless of where we are, and have a coffee. If we are out we find a cafe. Got to have that 11.00am coffee!

1.00pm - Lunch time - for those not at school.

4.00pm - Time for a snack. When we got home from school we normally had a slice of bread with dripping and salt.

5.30pm - Tea time or supper. This was sandwiches, jam mostly, and cake if we were lucky. Tidy up toys: we only had a few so it didn't take long.

6.00pm - Bath time and the start of bed time for the youngest children. In the summer, some of us bathed in a tin bath in the garden.

7.00pm - 8.00pm - The rest of the school children were put to bed. This never changed, except when we went to the Deaf Club. Deaf Club was open every Saturday.

8.00pm to 11.00pm - Various tasks including knitting clothes for us, ironing and preparing for the next day.

With the youngest two children her routine slowed down a little, as she had a washing machine and some of us had moved out or were more independent.

It must have been lonely for her, the only time she signed was with Daddy at the 11.00am coffee time. Occasionally, her best friend from Deaf school, Irene, would come for a cup of tea. There wasn't a phone, a

We Are CODA

Mummy With Madeleine And Julian

television or a radio until much later, although none of these would have been useful to her anyway.

Until now, I never thought of how lonely it must have been for Mummy, when we went for picnics, or to the cinema, she never had a friend who would join us, with their children. Mummy often went to see Mrs Fincham, her whole family were Deaf, including their children; we would all play in the street.

If you try for one day, not to have any communication with anyone, not to speak! Would you cope, could you manage living in a silent world with just children to communicate with! I know I couldn't cope, even having the TV on during the day without sound, it is better than having no visual stimulation.

Other Mummy Stories

I can remember winter times walking back from school. If I had used my bus fare for a bread roll at the baker's next to the school, my knees would get so cold with the wind, as I didn't have tights and the walk home was just over a mile. My knees were so painful. Mummy would be by the door waiting to rub Vaseline® on my knees, which hurt too!

We would line up in the kitchen each morning have a spoonful of malt, (which we loved) and cod liver oil, (which tasted awful). Even today, I have a daily spoonful of malt and cod liver oil.

When we were babies, Mummy would take us for our first year to the baby clinic. She would pile us in the pram and off we would go. Baby clinics were usually an opportunity to meet and chat with other mothers, but Mummy never did. The nurse would just smile and point and nod or shake her head. The only time she could communicate in her first language, Sign Language, was at the Cambridge Deaf Club, which was open every Saturday, but she didn't go on a regular basis until we were older.

The few times Mummy was sent to a 'Convalescent Home' for a rest, the older girls (and sometimes an aunt) looked after us. Even in the home, she had no one to communicate with. It must have been frustrating for her, as an intelligent woman, to have people over-exaggerate words and gestures to try and communicate. She showed great patience with these people.

Mummy would sometimes take the pram and fill it with old clothes (shirts, dresses, jumpers - anything else she thought was good quality) from jumble sales. From these treasures, she created new clothes for all of us. She was incredibly skilled at sewing beautiful dresses for my sisters and me, plus trousers and shirts for my brothers.

Both Mummy and Daddy designed their own outfits, from their own patterns, making stylish attire. They were always meticulous about how we looked when we went out - our clothes had to be neat and our shoes polished.

The Cruel World of Dementia

Being Deaf with Dementia was hell for us as a family. It was hard to see Mummy turn from an active and funny Deaf woman, the 'matriarch' of our family, to a confused, angry, scared and lost person. Not knowing who she was, was so heart breaking for us all and for

Daddy. Mummy was diagnosed with Alzheimer's when she was about 70 years old, and suffered with the disease for about thirteen years, which I understand is longer than normal.

I feel we all noticed Mummy change at different times and in different ways. Mummy went to one of my sister's for lunch, which she did often. It was not far, about a twenty-minute walk. Mummy was supposed to arrive at the normal time, but didn't arrive until a few hours later, looking a bit unwell. She signed, *"Lost"* with a confused facial expression, which my sister has never forgotten. She finds it very difficult to talk about it. As we all do.

Gabrielle noticed her change when they were on a barge holiday, which they had been on before. Gabby said Mummy looked confused and didn't seem to know what we were signing. The holiday was spent keeping Mummy safe and ensuring she didn't wander around too much, which was difficult on a barge.

I first noticed when I popped in to see Mummy and Daddy. Daddy looked worried and signed, *"Something wrong Mummy."* I can still see myself kneeling on the floor next to Mummy. She was smiling, but I couldn't see anything in her eyes, it was as if there was nothing there. I tapped Mummy's arm and asked her name *"Name Eileen?"* I signed. She smiled and nodded.

I signed, *"Fingerspell name."*

She looked at me and fingerspelled, *"Ei"* and then looked as if she was trying so hard to remember. She looked at me with a scared face and shrugged her shoulders, she couldn't remember. I hugged her.

I signed, *"Don't worry,"* and hugged them both. When I was outside, I sobbed. How were we going to cope? How was she going to manage and was she going to be able to stay safe?

What I didn't know at the time was the person with Dementia, doesn't know they have the disease and doesn't realise the impact their illness has on their family. I know there were times when Mummy was confused and would look scared.

Mummy was taken to get her test results and they came back as we all thought - she was suffering with Alzheimer's. When I asked Mummy's doctor about the type of dementia, he explained it as, *"The blood supply going through to her brain, was like a kettle which had furred up and water couldn't get through."* Personally, I felt her body was just worn out.

I clearly remember popping over to their house to see them, and Mummy wasn't there. Daddy sat looking so miserable, I signed, *"Mummy where?"* The Community Worker from the Deaf Club had come over with a minibus and taken Mummy to the Deaf Club, to give Daddy a break. I was furious. Daddy had not been told they were coming. They just turned up, put Mummy's hat and coat on and left. He didn't know what time they were coming back. He was lonely without his wife and wanted to spend as much time as possible with her, as he knew she was going to go into a care home. Putting it lightly, they never took Mummy again!

The landlords of The Rock, our local pub, knew our family well as we have used the pub as a family gathering

Mummy

place for many years. On one occasion, they phoned to let us know Mummy was in the pub, with a coat on, a shoe on one foot and a slipper on the other, taking sips from customers drinks. One of my siblings shot round there and took Mummy home. Daddy had fallen asleep and had forgotten to lock the front door.

Mummy's illness took its toll very slowly. After many years we were all exhausted and emotionally drained. We supported Daddy as well as Mummy, as he was not well. When I was younger, I had said to myself, if anything happened to our parents, I would want to live with them and look after them. However, in reality, this was not possible, as is often the case. I had my own children, my own home and job I needed to feed and clothe my children and pay their school fees.

A few years prior, one of my brothers purchased our parents' council house and built an annexe on the side. The annexe was perfect for them. Yet, we couldn't expect him to look after our parents 24/7, nor did we want him too. We all struggled with the situation: to keep Mummy safe and at the same time ensure Daddy was cared for.

Sometimes, I look back at those heart-breaking times and think how difficult it must have been for Mummy, she had always lived in a silent world but she could communicate through Sign Language, had lots of friends and such a full life and now this cruel illness!

When I went to the Deaf Club, her friends asked what was wrong with her. She looked different and unable to sign or communicate. This was a time when Dementia was not really understood or discussed. It was just seen as an ageing disease. Her Deaf friends could not see what was wrong, as the illness was not visual and they felt it was strange she had changed. I explained Mummy was ill of the mind, not of the body and her brain was worn out. Some of the older Deaf people still did not understand and just shrugged their shoulders. A few of them even signed, *"Mother stupid."* Now, thank goodness, we are all (Deaf and hearing) more aware of Dementia. Dementia awareness adverts are on TV and on social media. These adverts however only show hearing people with Dementia, more work needs to be done to show Deaf people with Dementia and across a wider spectrum of society.

Mummy no longer had a way to communicate. Her mind had deteriorated, her signing had disappeared, her love for her husband, children and her friends had gone. All we had left was a shell. No smiles, no hugs, no recognition, it couldn't get any worse. Mummy was gone, but not gone! A gut-wrenching and tearful realisation for us all.

My grandmother (Mum) died when she was 98 years old. Mummy was still alive at her death and was in the beginning of Alzheimer's. At the funeral, Mummy was in the front row, with her sisters. She was smiling unable to understanding what was going on which was sad for us all.

One winter, Mummy had two assessments at Fulbourn Mental Hospital (now called Fulbourn Hospital) near Cambridge. I drove Mummy there and I had no idea of the process or how she would react when I dropped

Mummy

her off. I was not emotionally prepared for her reaction and it did not occur to me that she would be so scared.

Once inside, I wanted to turn around and take Mummy straight back out with me. The hospital needed to do the assessment without the family around so as not to give a false assessment of her needs. As a family we would have automatically stepped in and assisted her and them. I stayed with Mummy whilst the staff booked her in: all seemed okay and the male nurse was kind. They knew she was Deaf and said not to worry, they would look after her. I gave Mummy a hug goodbye and smiled, while inside I was crying, I knew I mustn't let her see how upset I was, but I couldn't fool her, she knew from my facial expressions.

Just as I was going to leave, Mummy grabbed hold me. She was petrified, holding on to my arm, shaking her head and trying to scream. I knew she wanted me to take her away. My hands shook; I was still trying to smile, signing, *"It's okay, don't worry, nurse look after you."* It may have been better for Mummy if the nurse had been female. She might have felt less scared. The male nurse held Mummy gently and was nice. Mummy was clinging to me and making a fearful noise, begging with her eyes, *"Don't leave me."* Against all my instincts, to grab Mummy, run to the car and to take her home. I gently took her hands off me and kept smiling while I walked away, hearing her making that awful sound. This took place over thirty years ago and inside I still feel it was yesterday.

After her assessment, it was decided Mummy would need to go into full-time care as Daddy was unable to look after her, even with family support.

Moving Into The Care Home

I was with Daddy while two siblings packed Mummy's suitcase with clothes and dolls (she had come to hug them - a possible faint reminder of when she had babies) to take her to the care home.

The care home she was taken to was beautiful. We couldn't have wished for better for her. It was in Magrath Avenue, Cambridge where there had been an old cinema, The Rex Cinema, and also The Rendezvous, a night club (where Nickolas had been on stage with The Rolling Stones). When The Rex was demolished they built a care home run by a Housing Association. The care home has now closed, and it is a block of flats.

The day after Mummy was taken to the care home, I went to see her. The staff were lovely and had bought a Sign Language book so they could learn to sign to her. I explained hearing with dementia still can communicate with their voice, they may not make much sense but could communicate on some level. Mummy's form of communication was physical, but she had forgotten what signs meant and even how to sign. We could not have asked for better care and staff, Mummy had her own room, which we decorated. When I visited her, she would normally be sitting in her room or in the lounge with a doll on her lap.

My siblings and myself were able to visit her anytime, even late at night just to see her. I would often creep into her room to give her kiss. I knew Mummy wasn't

Mummy

aware; I did it partly for my own comfort, always hoping for some response. One afternoon, my youngest sister, Francesca, and I went to visit her, she was sitting in her armchair with a doll on her lap. I thought, 'blow this', I took the doll off her lap, sat on the floor beside her and put my head on her lap. Mummy hugged my head tightly, I was in a vice grip and could not move. I called out for Francesca to help me but she couldn't as she was laughing so much!

After Mummy had moved into the care home, I had changed jobs and started work at The Royal School for the Deaf, Derby as Residential Manager. I clearly remember July 15th 1998. At 3.15pm, the receptionist at the school said there was a phone call for me. One of my sisters had called and said, *"Mummy died this afternoon."* I collapsed on the floor. The school secretary and receptionist were wonderful and took care of me. Fortunately, I lived on site and could prepare a bag ready for my daughter, Dominique, to pick me up. All I can remember doing was sob: Mummy was gone.

Dominique drove me to Cambridge to meet the rest of my siblings. My sister phoned again while I was in the car to let me know Mummy had to have an autopsy as she hadn't seen a doctor within three days. I asked Dominique to pull over while I vomited: the thought of Mummy being cut up was more than I could bear.

When it came to organising the funeral, particularly the flowers and what Mummy was going to wear, it fell upon my sisters and I. We could not agree on what Mummy should wear. I said, *"Her pinafore, as she was always wearing it."* My older sisters said, *"She hated that pinafore, she will wear her kaftan."* I was so upset; I didn't realise Mummy hated her pinny so much! How naive was I?

Many of our 'Deaf Family' came to her funeral. We had no interpreter, but it didn't seem important. It was just lovely to see so many people there. Mummy was cremated and her ashes were put under the William Pear tree in the back garden at the family home, where she would rest with Daddy.

Mummy

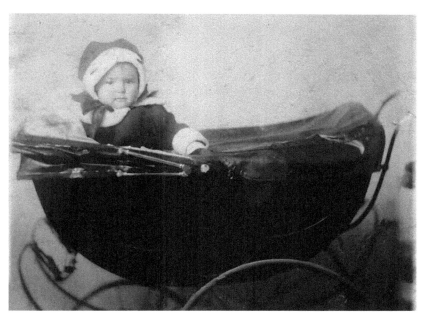

Our Grandfather, Carried This Photo of Mummy With Him Throughout WWI

We Are CODA

*Back Row: Louisa Hempstead, John Hempstead, Yvonne Sibellas,
Daddy and Mummy, Ethel Sibellas, Claudius Sibellas and Mabel
Front Row: Pauline Sibellas, (unknown boy), Josette Sibellas, Maureen Sibellas*

*Day Out In Margate, 1936; Wedding Day, 1937
Day Out, 1978 And Dancing, 1983*

We Are CODA

Daddy Sewing, Using His Famous Invisible Mending Technique.

Daddy
William Sydney
Hempstead
1912 - 1996

Daddy was born in 1912 in Cambridge. He was given the names William Sidney. He was the middle child of Annetta and William a financially poor family. He had two sisters, both hearing, Nora and Violet. They lived near the Gas Works in Cambridge.

We know little about his father, other than he had a poor relationship with him. Daddy described him as a 'drinker'. Daddy's father was not from a good family and was thrown out by his mother and grandmother. He rarely mentioned his father or his paternal grandparents. I know his paternal grandmother was called Martha and had been reported in the local paper for having a street fight with another woman. Daddy would have hated the thought of his grandmother fighting: he would have thought it very common. However, Daddy would talk affectionately about his mother and how much he loved her.

Daddy went to a hearing school in Young Street, Cambridge, which has since closed, before he was sent to the Royal School for Deaf and Dumb Children, Margate. The word Dumb was dropped in the early 1970s. At seven years old it was his first time away from his mother and from home. I often wonder if he knew where he was going when his mother took him to the railway station? Had she told him and had he been on a train before? I wish I had asked him.

He said his wonderful, kind mother, whom he loved dearly, would accompany a group of Deaf children from Cambridge to Margate by train at the beginning of each term and make the same trip to collect them at the end of each term.

Daddy told us little about his school life, but he did say school was cruel at times. He was put in a class with children who were less able. The child was judged not on their ability, but on whether they were more 'oral' and used less Sign Language as their main form of communication.

At the age of 21, his mother died and Daddy went to live with his grandmother. She was a tiny lady under five feet tall and always wore layer upon layer of black clothing and was one of sixteen children, which was not unusual in the late 19th and early 20th centuries.

Daddy informed his grandmother he had been seeing a young Deaf girl, Eileen Sibellas: he loved her and he was going to marry her. His grandmother was furious, she didn't want him to marry a Deaf girl, he was to marry a hearing girl, not a Deaf girl. She had threatened, *"If you marry her, I won't leave you anything in my will or any money."* Daddy was so upset, as he loved his grandmother (she was all he had when his mother died) yet his love for Mummy was stronger.

Daddy was good at everything he did and he proved this in later life. He made our bunk beds, a rocking horse, a dolls house out of a drawer with lights, a Summer House, a canoe, our coats, dressing gowns, his own clothes and won awards for competitions against Deaf and hearing competitors in swimming and chess.

Daddy made most of his clothes. He would go into the Cambridge town centre wearing a black cloak, deerstalker and with his groomed long beard and hair; he really stood out from the crowd. Sometimes people would make fun of him calling him 'Rumpelstiltskin' and laugh. He didn't let it show, he was a proud man, but he felt every word. It also upset those of us who went to town with him. Even though he did not know exactly what they were saying, he felt for us as he knew it was unkind. He would look down and grip our hand tighter, with a wonderful warm and loving smile. We knew he was saying, *"Be proud!"* and we were. But we did also have tears.

Daddy said his favourite hobbies at school were swimming, art and chess. Daddy made lifelong friends at school: most Deaf children who have attended Deaf Residential schools end up having lifelong friends from these times.

For this chapter, I knew I needed to do research and start looking through my vast number of archives, and I am glad I did! I found the memoirs of Daddy's life he had asked me to write down for him. It was titled,

We Are CODA

Daddy Playing Chess

My Life, dated 18th June 1987. I wrote it in Daddy's own BSL English.

Daddy and I spent an afternoon with him signing to me while I wrote in longhand. It was not easy to watch him sign while writing. There were many times, I used the sign, *"Hold"* which frustrated him. Daddy was not always a patient man and he would sign, *"Hurry up."* There are times when I look back and become cross with myself asking myself, *"Why didn't I type up his memories while he was still here? Why did I wait until after his death in 1996?"*

After I finished writing, I asked why he had asked me write down his memoirs? He replied my signing was good, like a Deaf person, better than my brothers and sisters. I was so chuffed and proud, so of course I had to tell my siblings!

As mentioned, the memoir was written in Daddy's English and in British Sign Language English (English was Daddy's second language). Rather than myself explain the meaning of BSL English, it is culturally more acceptable for me ask a Deaf person. On asking a Deaf friend, their reply was, "Each BSL sign does not correspond with each English word. BSL is a visual language with facial expressions, Body Language and gestures. To write in BSL English means you write how you structure your signs. In English, one would write or say, 'What is your name?' To write in BSL English it would show as, 'Your name what?' Signing in BSL, using BSL structure, it is 'Name what?' with facial expressions to show it is a question."

'My Life' as signed by William Hempstead

"I born Cambridge, 10 Gas Lane in 1912. Realise that I was Deaf when 3 years old. I went Young Street, Cambridge when 5 years, sent me Royal School for the Deaf Margate in 1918, when I was seven. I left school when 16 years old and went Co-op in Cambridge and work tailor. I learned tailoring at School for the Deaf when I was 14 years old. I made my own clothes from materials provided by school; this was pinstripe cloth and made my suit. My teacher for tailoring came to Cambridge and saw I working as a tailor and was very proud of me. His name was Mr. Peter, unfortunately he is dead now.

At school I good at art and painting and won three certificates. It was suggested went to Technical College study art and painting but told too many artists in Cambridge and they suggested I went private and

We Are CODA

Still Life Paintings by William Hempstead

Daddy

paid for myself. This was £12.00 per term for lesson, I had no money and there was no one to pay for me. They told me that my paintings were excellent, but sometimes the clients were not nice and so I gave that up and went to work the Co-op in Burleigh Street as a tailor. This was a high-class shop where the Co-op asked me to clean windows. I asked them why; they said my work at making suits was closed and were now being to the factory to be made. Told them I would not do that, I was a tailor and I left the Co-op to work for myself, it is now 1948.

My hobby at time and been for long time was swimming and I was member of ASA, but I left Cambridge ASA and organised my own swimming club called the Granta Swimming Club. I was the

Queen Elizabeth II by William Hempstead

Treasurer and also Captain for the relays and water polo. I had good times. There were many matches at the Leys School, at Jesus Green, Yarmouth and Royston Lagoon swimming pool. These were marvellous times.

I still did my painting, mostly use oils and refused to take other artists along. I was presented with a certificate when at school, 12 years old by the Prince of Wales I still have this certificate at home. Once a policeman came to my house and told me not to paint, I showed him my certificate that I got from school. They didn't know about this.

I worked as a tailor from 14 years old for 45 years, a bit too long. There was no one to support me, to help me. I need a rest but no one comes, so I work, like a workaholic, work, work, work. Why do people come and ask for help? Today, people don't learn to sew or alter things, they come from all over the world. U.S.A., Vietnam, Germany, Belgians, Saudi Arabians, even Egyptians.

Egypt, where we had a marvellous time - you never believe me, I have some photos in an album. In Spain, Egypt, Greece, I have some knowledge there I don't know why, but thanks to British passports, British sail ports, Cambridge Board. Thank God we are British. It is really by good human aid kindness, everybody trusts the friendliness, no enemies. We are born in the world is nothing to some, not to be afraid of if any illness comes. It is up to us care for the world, don't let the world have wars.

Daddy

This is all I can say on freedom. It is not matter if we are born rich or poor, but we must be honest to Queen or King or next of kin. I have to work to help my families, giving in skills, I am Deaf, no matter about that. Must work as your life needs you. Thinks, machine, needles, cottons, material, people need them to keep covered and warm."

Looking back at these happy memories of Daddy's, I think how wonderful he was and what a strong influence he had on my connection with the Deaf Community.

Top: Daddy On A Camel, Egypt
Bottom: Mummy On A Camel, Egypt

We Are CODA

Daddy In Scarborough For A Chess Tournament, 1939

More Stories About Daddy

Daddy was eccentric, dressed very dapper and believed we should all do the right thing and never break the law. Daddy always went back to tailoring as he was always in demand. He finally stopped when he was in his late sixties or early seventies. I know he had a few retirement parties.

Joining the Army

As family legend goes, during World War Two, Daddy decided to sign up for the army, so off he went to the recruiting office to sign up to fight in the war. He came back angry, saying they cheated him, and it was not fair. He had gone into the recruitment office, stood in front of the recruitment officer and said he wanted to join to fight in the War. Maybe his speech was unclear, and they did not understand him, or possibly he didn't understand what the officer was saying. Daddy was quite good at lip-reading so did the officer lower his head to speak knowing Daddy couldn't hear? A soldier came into the room while my father was standing by the officer's desk and stood behind my father and dropped a tin tray (a tin tray makes a high pitch clang sound). Obviously, Daddy did not move or even twitch, and I can assure you a 'tin tray' is very loud. The officer told my Daddy, *"Sorry can't join the Army as you are Deaf."* This is why Daddy came back saying they cheated him. I love this story, some Deaf people were recruited to lip-read and to work in factories which were so loud they would have destroyed a hearing person's hearing.

Daddy Driving

Daddy was so happy when he received his Provisional Driving Licence in 1960, (I still have it in my suitcase of bits of paper) he was excited about the thought of going to get a car and take his family on 'Days Out'. When Daddy was learning to drive, he used Uncle Tom's car and about six of us would clamber in the back and fight over who was going to hang their head out of the window! It was an old black Ford, which had leather seats and no seat belts.

Uncle Tom was Daddy's brother-in-law and he couldn't sign. I am not sure how many driving lessons Daddy had. When the day came for him to take his driving test, Uncle Tom was ill, so Daddy decided to drive himself!

When he got to the Driving Test Centre, he was asked where the driving instructor was. Daddy told them that his Driving Instructor was ill so he had driven himself. He didn't know it would mean he was put down as an 'automatic fail' and the police were sent to our house. Daddy never had any more driving lessons or ever talked about wanting to drive.

Daddy was scared of the police, I'm not sure why. When one brother got into trouble with the police due to a motorbike issue, the police came to the house which made Daddy so angry. My brother has never forgotten how upset he was. Daddy had signed, *"Leave house, not good bring police our house."*

At Our Local

Many Deaf men used to be called 'Dummy' by hearing people, which was seen as acceptable at the time. Some people would call Daddy, 'Dummy Tailor', but it didn't seem to bother him. The Rock, on Cherry Hinton Road, was our local pub and Daddy would visit on many occasions.

On one of his visits some young hearing guys were teasing him because he was Deaf, they were making grunting noises and flinging their arms around, thinking it was funny. Well, Daddy soon showed them it wasn't funny. They got black eyes and Daddy got to finish his pint in peace. Most of the time Daddy would just walk away, but this time they were interfering with his pint.

Home Life

Daddy always loved a bargain (or what he thought was a bargain). He would come home with the strangest objects, which did not work or were awful. We would sign, *"Where from?"* with an exasperated look on our faces. If we did say anything he would get very cross and sign, *"Mind your own business!"* which is one of my favourite signs. Even a person without sign would understand the meaning.

Mummy would always tell him to get rid of his latest 'bargain'. He wouldn't and sometimes it would end up hidden in the vegetable garden or at the bottom of the garden. Daddy would grow most of the vegetables and kept chickens (many families did at the time). Later, he made a greenhouse, out of polythene, which he would spend hours pottering around in.

When we were children, he made us many toys for the garden, he adapted old bikes to make carts, pulling trolleys, tents, paddling pools, canoes; anything he could make into a toy for us he did. He took the wheels of the old Silver Cross® pram which was used for most of us as babies and made it into see-saw.

Daddy's recollection of meeting Mummy

He was with friends, signing away, and the front door opened. A big man with red hair and a bushy moustache entered with a very pretty, shy girl, clutching his hand. Daddy said the minute he saw her, he really liked her. He smiled and signed for them both to come in. The man, her father, could not sign, he just smiled trying to get Mummy to come in. That first time, she just wouldn't come in!

When Mummy returned a few years later, she and Daddy 'paired off' almost straight away. Most of the young Deaf boys liked Mummy and would try and get her to sit on their lap. Mummy only had eyes for Daddy. Maybe if she had known they would have had ten hearing children, she would have thought twice!

Daddy covered most of his life in the interview I had with him, but there was so much more to him. If he was alive today in the world of social media, there would have been many photos of him online, with very positive comments about his look, his long white hair and beard and about his self-made clothes.

Researching

Children seem to think they know everything about their parents, their lives, their friends, and their interests and beliefs, but of course they don't. Through my research as part of Cambridge Deaf Association, I found a photo of Daddy dating back to about 1928. He is with a group of Deaf people, who I also recognised. The men are wearing sashes with letters on them and a badge, medal or emblem at the bottom. None of my sisters or I had seen the photo before, even Gabrielle was quite surprised. Francesca did some research about the photo and found some very interesting facts. It made us think, *'Wow! None of us knew anything about this.'*

Experts who have looked at the photo, have claimed the sashes are not military but Masonic. The DC on the sash of the man in the middle stands for 'Director of Ceremonies'.

However, the tradition in many branches of Freemasonry, such as the Craft Masons and the Holy Arch Chapter - is to wear an apron alongside the sash, which these do not. The experts went on to say, it is possible these men were members of a Knights Templar branch of Freemasonry, and my sister Francesca, could investigate further by contacting the Freemasons Grand Lodge to try and learn about the figures in the photo. We were curious as to why Daddy would join the Freemasons.

Our conversation circled round to, *"Maybe, it was too much to pay for a yearly subscription to the Freemasons"*, *"Was Daddy initiated into the Lodge as the Grand Master there?"* From what we knew of Daddy it seemed unlikely he would have joined them.

Daddy's Interests

Daddy was a very intelligent man, he knew a lot about the world and would read a newspaper from front to back every day, he loved knowing about what was going on and had many discussions with his Deaf friends at the Saturday Deaf Club, where the men would get together and chat about politics.

Deaf Olympics

Daddy's main love was swimming. He was a founding member of the Granta Swimming Club and was very much respected there. I don't think they ever knew he had won a Bronze Medal, in the Deaf Olympics, in 1939.

Sadly, the Bronze Medal was stolen from the house many years ago. We are still trying to find what the medal looked like.

John Hay, a Deaf Historian, visited Deaf Clubs and Centres around England, with clips of films which had been given to him by Deaf people. John Hay's role was to find anyone who could recognised people from these videos. I was visiting Peterborough Deaf Club the day John did. How lucky was I?!

Everyone was excited about the clips, recognising old friends, families and places. When John showed a clip of the 1939 Deaf Olympics, I was the one who got most excited. I jumped up and signed, *"My Daddy!"* The clip showed Daddy walking in the Deaf Olympics Parade. I cried.

He won his Bronze Medal in the 'freestyle' category. Gold and Silver were won by two German contestants.

The 1939 Deaf Olympics was the fifth such event known as the 'International Silent Games'. It was held in Stockholm, Sweden between 24-27th August: thirteen countries participated. The Second World War started four days later.

Previously, Daddy had told us, due to the talk about the start of War, the Deaf Olympics had to finish early. All athletes were told, *"Do not discuss anything about the War. Keep quiet and don't talk to anyone outside, keep safe."* They all had to pack up and go back to their own countries.

Deaf Club Times

Daddy loved playing games and entertaining children, especially his own. At the Deaf Club he would dress up as Father Christmas, be a Magician and a Ventriloquist!

When I tell hearing people my Deaf father was a Ventriloquist, they look at me with a confused look as if to say how? He used to have what was called a 'dummy' on his lap, perhaps it is politically correct to now say puppet. Daddy made the puppet: it was a black puppet, three feet tall and had a fake cigarette hanging out of its big red lips. Its suit was black with a white shirt and a green felt hat with a red and white band.

Daddy would have his hand in the back of the puppet and sign to it with one hand. He really made it look as if the puppet understood him and then look at us. We all thought it very funny, even writing this now I am giggling to myself.

When he was on the stage as a Magician he was dressed in a long black cloak with white lining and a

Deaflympics

Daddy

Daddy with Awards from Granta Swimming Club, 1934

William Sidney HEMPSTEAD

Games	Sport	Event	Result
Stockholm 1939	Swimming	1500m freestyle	**Bronze**

Great Britain

Born: 4 Apr 1912

Gender: M

Official Deaflympics Record For 1939

119

stand up collar, His bow tie was white; he had a top hat and a magician's wand. He made it all himself and of course the black suit he wore.

I remember two of his tricks. One was putting a white hanky through his ears, from one side he would be pushing the hanky through and put his head to the side as if he was trying to get the hanky through. Then he would pull the hanky out the other end. We would all sit there with our mouths open in awe. Over the years, this trick has been my favourite and I have played it on my grandchildren.

In the second trick I remember Daddy would always take something out of his top hat, like a hanky rabbit. One day, Daddy was very naughty and in front of

Daddy As Father Christmas With Gabrielle On The Left And Shaun Far Right Both In Stripy Jumpers Knitted By Family

*Daddy Playing The Knitting Game At The Deaf Club.
Mr Swallowe Is In The Grey Suit, One Person Behind Him.*

everyone at the Deaf Club, instead of pulling out a hanky bunny, he pulled out a pair of Mummy's knickers! Deaf people laughed so much. As children we didn't understand the hilarity. Mummy was furious, he never did it again.

British Deaf Association (BDA)

Daddy was very involved with the BDA and he is named in the book, *A Pictorial History of the BDA (1890-2015)* which was published to celebrate the 125th year of the BDA. Daddy was Secretary of the Cambridge Branch for a few years. Deaf people I meet today have remembered my father from years of him being involved in the Deaf Community. He always felt being Deaf was not a disability, being Deaf was a Culture and a Community.

Later Years

As Daddy became older, he started to lose his sight developing glaucoma and cataracts (possibly due to his work as a tailor). He would hold his newspaper to his face and hated being disturbed. Two of my sisters, would do a lot of his shopping, which would nearly always include a bottle of whisky. As Daddy's eyesight became worse, he would find it difficult to see signing if it wasn't right in front of him.

In 1996, Daddy started to struggle with his breathing so my brother Claudius took him to the doctors. The doctor recommended Daddy went to the hospital for tests; Claudius went with him. Claudius was also with Daddy when he was told the results: he had lung cancer. Claudius told Daddy about the cancer and the consultant asked him about chemotherapy. Daddy told Claudius, *"Tell him no, wife gone."* Claudius was then told, *"Your father has about six weeks left."* Claudius told Daddy, *"Not long live."* Daddy was okay about it.

All the siblings were spread around the world. It was a tough time for us all, but we all rallied around and helped with support from Macmillan nurses. Even some of the grandchildren helped. We had our rota written down and information about medication, appointments and visits. The nurses could not sign but they knew one of us would be around to help.

When Daddy needed to go to hospital, a few of us would go along sit in the waiting room in case we were needed to communicate for him. We would take turns, staying day and night if needed.

Daddy

On the day Daddy died, we were around his bed with the doctor and a Catholic priest. Only Francesca wasn't there (she was having a shower) when Daddy closed his eyes. The doctor put the stethoscope to his chest and said, *"He has gone."* The priest then said the Last Rites.

I found it traumatic and emotionally difficult. Daddy was not just my father, he was part of my Deaf Identity. He taught me so much about Deaf Culture and Community. He taught me basic American signs and fingerspelling: we had such a strong Deaf bond.

After the funeral, I was emotionally lost and exhausted driving back and forth to Derby, every week and trying to keep down a job, making sure the children were okay. I missed him so much and still do.

The day after Daddy died, Sebastian, my son, took Dominique, his sister to begin her course and new life at Nottingham University. I couldn't take her as I was too distraught. It was gut-wrenching for me to miss her important moment.

We Are CODA

My Extended Family

"I am many things: I am a woman, I am British Indian, I am a daughter, I am a sister, I am a friend, I am a teacher and I am a CODA. Being a Child of Deaf Adults is one of the biggest parts of me and has largely shaped who I am today."

**Diksha Shah,
Author, Dee's Stories: The Deaf Parents**

Extended Family

When I started on this book, I thought it best just to ask my brothers and sisters about their experience of having Deaf parents. Then one of my siblings said, *"You must talk to Auntie Maureen."* So I did! Auntie Maureen is the youngest sister of Mummy, she is now ninety-four years old. We have told her she can't die yet, and has to live at least another thirty years! Luckily, I have had the opportunity to ask her about what Mummy was like when she was a young girl. Mummy was fourteen when Auntie Maureen was born.

After talking to Auntie Maureen, I felt a bit sad thinking if Mummy had been hard-of-hearing (not Deaf), had mental health issues or been blind, would there have been more of an equal communication in their family? I love my aunt, she is funny, loud and has a variety of facial expressions which make me laugh.

Auntie Maureen's Memories

It was obvious to me as a young girl that my sister, Eileen, couldn't hear. I used to talk to her but she never replied. I don't think anyone specifically told me she was Deaf. I just knew or guessed. It was just the way she was. I think it has always been like that in our family, just accept the way things are, without asking why. I don't remember asking Mum or Dad why Eileen wouldn't talk to me.

When I was about ten years old, some children shouted at Eileen. They thought she was stupid because she couldn't hear. I was so angry. When I had finished with them, they regretted their comments.

I never found it difficult to communicate with her. A lot of people used gestures and 'lip patterns' but we all got round it one way or another.

Eileen and I would have a good laugh, I liked taking her out in the car saying everyone on the road is nuisance. She would kill herself with laughter. I think about my aunt's driving today, with great affection!

My last question to Auntie Maureen was, *"Did you ever think your Deaf sister, would have ten hearing children?"* She laughed, *"Well, none of us thought that."*

Extended Family

Billy Evans

I remember Billy Evans with wonderful, fond memories; we all do. Billy was a big part of my life from when I was a young child, he made me laugh and made Mummy happy, with his sense of humour and playful ways. He fitted in with all of us.

Billy Evans was young, tall, and very handsome (I thought) with white blonde hair and I have never forgotten his blonde eyebrows. Billy was our Deaf brother, we had Deaf parents but not a Deaf brother or sister. I was always amazed how he got into his mini car with his long legs: he seemed to fold himself in half, I would stand at the window and watch him with fascination.

Billy would come to our house and flirt with one of my sisters (which made Mummy laugh). She would go to Mummy and sign, *"Mummy you said Deaf with Deaf and hearing with hearing."* Mummy would reply, *"You same Deaf."* Billy really liked her and wanted to be her boyfriend, but she already had a boyfriend, but it never stopped Billy from flirting.

My parents loved him very much, he was such great fun and bought so much laughter to us all. Billy grew up at our house, I didn't even know if he had any parents or any brothers and sisters. I was told recently, he was an only child, and his parents were hearing. We wouldn't have asked him these questions as children. Billy was just there, at the Deaf Club, at Deaf outings and our house.

One day, Billy stopped coming to our house. I missed him. I would sit by the window and wait, looking forward for him to come and make Mummy and Daddy laugh. I remember tapping mummy on her arm and sign, *"Billy where?"* Mummy signed, *"Billy not coming, gone to heaven."* I was still confused. Gone to heaven, is what we learned at school when somebody good died, did this mean Billy had died? It was such a shock to me, I didn't realise people died! I didn't know how he died, or what it really meant. Our cat and dog had died but it wasn't too sad as I understood animals died.

One of my sisters became depressed after Billy died. She only told me recently: she didn't know she was grieving, she just felt sad all the time. Talking or discussing death and bereavement about the loss of someone you love was never bought up in our family. Feelings on how one felt when a loved one dies, was not something taught at school. We just became an unhappy house for a while.

When I spoke to my eldest brother about Billy Evans, a big smile came on his face. He remembered he and Billy use to play fight as brothers sometimes do. He asked me what happened to Billy: he had joined the army when Billy died and was never told. All he knew was when he came home on leave, Billy was not there.

Extended Family

He just thought Billy had got married or had a girlfriend or moved away. He was surprised when I told him Billy had died of cancer at 21. He wished he had known at the time.

You may wonder why I have included Billy Evans in the book. Simply, he was the first person in my extended Deaf Family who died. So many of my Deaf Family have now died and I find this emotionally difficult. I grew up with these people, went on Deaf outings with them, saw them at the Deaf Club and they were also the Deaf friends of my parents that visited our house.

We Are CODA

Linda Fincham

Linda was like our Deaf sister, similar to Billy Evans who we saw as our Deaf brother. Linda went to The Royal School for the Deaf Margate, she was born into a Deaf family. Mummy was very good friends with Linda's mother, Dorothy (who was also Deaf). They would visit each other's houses. Her grandparents, parents and her siblings were all Deaf. Her brother John married Fiona a Deaf woman, they have hearing children and grandchildren. Linda, had one son, who is hearing. Her son's father was hearing. Linda's grandchildren are hearing as well. Ann her sister never had children.

When Mummy started to have more free time, Linda, Irene Hunt and Mummy would spend time together at the 'Catholic Club', which was open on Saturday nights. Many a Saturday night has been with the three dancing away, after a few drinks! They were well known for putting their hands on the 'Juke Box' or feel the floor vibrate to get them dancing. Linda was a very good dancer. At times, my sisters and I joined them on these nights out.

Linda and I would visit Deaf clubs in Norwich, Bury St Edmunds, Ipswich and of course Cambridge.

Sometimes Deaf people we met would ask if we were sisters as we were so close and got the giggles often, it was as if we knew what the other was thinking. I spent many hours at Linda's house in Cambridge helping her with the gardening and other tasks. I also remember her having many cats!

I still meet with Deaf people who went to Margate Deaf School with Linda, and knew her brother and sister. John Fincham and I are in the Cambridge Deaf Club History Society. We are preparing a celebration of one hundred years of the Cambridge Deaf Club, which will be held in 2027. If Linda was still with us, she would have joined the group.

One of my sisters told me of her time spent with Linda when she worked as a Community Worker at Cambridge Deaf Centre. They would have trips out together. On one of their trips, Linda had won a competition to visit the 'Coronation Street' set in Birmingham. Both of them went up by train, stayed overnight at a hotel and had all expenses paid. They met the cast, had dinner with Barbara Knox (she played the part of Rita). My sister said, "We had a really good time and a great laugh."

Before I moved to Derby in 1995, Linda and I organised 'Deaf and hearing groups' at Cambridge Deaf Club, we held them about once a month. We played Deaf games and had such a laugh. It was also an opportunity for hearing students who were learning BSL to mix with Deaf people.

Linda was on the CDA Committee for many years, ensuring the Deaf Club always served Deaf People and had Deaf people involved in all decisions. She did have a fight on her hands at times. Linda was strong and never gave up.

It was such a lovely surprise to find out that Cambridge Deaf Club, which has always be known as 'Hope Hall' was changed to 'Fincham House' in memory of Linda, in November 2022. She would have been so happy to know that all her hard work was appreciated.

I miss Linda, my sisters and I still talk about her with such fondness and laugh about the good, and naughty, times we had with her.

Extended Family

Paul Sibellas

My cousin, Paul, spent a lot of time with us as children. Even today we are all very close, which is nice. Paul's mother was the third sister of Mummy, her name was Pauline. Auntie Pauline had two children, Paul was her first and Grainne, her second. Grainne stayed with us as well. It just seemed that our cousins loved staying with us and going to the seaside together.

There are many old photos of our cousins with us, even before I was born, on the beach, mostly in North Norfolk.

I can remember clearly when I first saw Grainne as a baby, my heart glowed for my Auntie Pauline, what a wonderful woman to have adopted a Black baby. I'm sure Mummy told us that Grainne was adopted! But as a young child, I would not have known what the sign for adopt was or how to spell the word 'adopt'. Maybe it was an older sibling that told me! Anyway, Grainne wasn't adopted, she was Paul's half-sister.

Paul's Memories

I grew up knowing my aunt and uncle couldn't hear. I don't remember any starting point when I was told. I may have been told or just worked it out for myself.

As far as I can remember, no one in the family ever said anything as there was nothing to say.

When I visited the Hempsteads it was like a switch turned on: I just knew I could not speak normally, but need to communicate with gestures. I just got on with it. If I got stuck, I would ask one of my cousins to sign or fingerspell for me. The only problem with that was they were such jokers. If I asked, I knew one of them would sign or fingerspell something very different. I got caught out a lot. I knew when something wasn't right as Auntie Eileen would give me a strange look or just laugh. Also, the cousin I had asked for help would run off laughing. I never signed fully: I didn't know how, but I would try and communicate by moving my lips clearly and make some signs myself. I knew how to sign my sign for drink, food, bye, hello, just basic stuff. I enjoyed spending time with Auntie Eileen and Uncle William and using my own way of communication. I was never embarrassed about them being Deaf.

Sebastian

My relationship with my grandparents as a young boy was somewhat shaped by the fact that they were Deaf and I couldn't sign very well. We relied heavily on lip reading and hand gestures to communicate which limited what we talked about. We didn't really discuss the finer things in life, but then I guess many young children have this with their grandparents, regardless of hearing ability. Despite all of this, I always felt loved in their presence.

Grandpa was very funny and mischievous, and Grandma was always gentle and caring. My Grandpa taught me how to play chess, I was about ten years old and he taught me how to play to 'County Level' where I played in a tournament. Grandpa had won many awards countrywide as a Chess Player, he played against Deaf and hearing people. I was taught through lots of taps on the table with facial expressions, hand gestures and thumbs up and down!

My sister and I would stay over a lot on Friday evenings when my mother went to work. I didn't always like the sleepovers; part of the issue was the fact that I was never allowed to choose what to watch. My Grandpa always dominated the small, boxy, poor-quality TV and his favourite programme was snooker. My TV aggravation became more prominent as the volume was either off or very low and the remote control was always being out of reach: it belonged to Grandpa!

Alone at night, I was more conscious of my grandparent's deafness. I was the only one hearing the strange creaks and groans of the house. At the same time, I was overlooked by my grandmother's collection of dolls, which seemed to take on a presence more like Stephen King's, *IT,* in a dark room with a shaft of light cutting across their faces! The house itself felt slightly dark, complemented by slightly dark furniture.

My mum recalls her brothers and sisters preferring the dark and not needing to put lights on in the house. She also says, Bella, her eldest granddaughter finds it very odd that she can sit in the dark watching TV with subtitles.

But the kitchen at the back of the house was always light. It's where my grandfather weaned me onto homemade piccalilli sauce on thick, chunky sandwiches or, for a real treat, lemon curd on floppy white slices of bread. It's also where my grandmother simmered Coca-Cola® as her homemade remedy for stomach-ache. It worked, but I have no idea how she came up with it.

The living room was full of artwork painted by my grandfather. He had painted two of my mother, when she was a young girl, other family members, the Pyramids and Royal Family. There was a particularly lovely portrait of Queen Elizabeth II when she was young. There was even a very long painting of a nude

Extended Family

woman! I did wonder if it was my Grandma (I hoped not). Many years later, my mother told me the face was Grandma and Grandpa used his own imagination for the body!

Off the hallway on the left near the front door was my Grandpa's sewing workroom. He was a tailor, and often I would hear the whirs and clicks of his foot pedalled black Singer® sewing machine. When his customers would come to the door to either give him work or collect the work he had completed, they would press the bell at the front door. When the bell was pressed, it didn't ring; instead all the lights in the house would dim. This was new technology for Deaf people, which was great.

My grandparents' house was used as the gathering spot for the wider family. As they had ten children, spending time there with numerous aunties, uncles and cousins made for the best summer days.

Often, we would head to Cambridge Deaf Club. These were always fun occasions with rowdy children running around the place, we were less restricted never being told, 'Keep the noise down', we loved it. The Deaf Club was a mix of Deaf and hearing people with lots of laughter as one would expect in such a close-knit community.

I do remember being in a pub with one of my cousins, Alexandra, and saw a girl I thought was attractive. Alexandra had already passed her Level I in British Sign Language, which meant we were able to sign to each other, well basic signing from my part, and I signed, "She is pretty." The girl looked and me and signed,

139

"Thank you!" I was so embarrassed, but I did get to chat to her.

Sadly, my Grandma slipped into Dementia, and was moved into a Care Home, they were wonderful to her and looked after her well. My last memory of my Grandpa was his wit and spirit. During my last visit to see him, despite his age (he was in his eighties) and bed-bound by cancer, he still had his humour. When the nurse who was looking after him at the time turned away to give us some time on our own, Grandpa looked at me, sculptured his hands in an 'hourglass shape' in the air, his cheeks puffed out and his eyes smiled. This was him using Sign Language to say the nurse had a rather attractive figure.

I loved my grandparents, they were kind, loving and always signed to me. My mother over the years had taught me the alphabet and quite a few 'home signs'. With both of them being Deaf, it helped me.

Grandpa, 1991

Extended Family

Dominique

Dominique told me she loved writing for the book and how wonderful it was wonderful to read my family's stories, emotional but in a good way.

Dominique's memories

I have always been incredibly proud of my upbringing and background. I don't think I realised how unique and special my family was, and still is, until now. I have fond memories of spending time at my Deaf grandparents' house as a child. There was always so much family around which made me feel safe and secure.

My Grandma used to always feed me with lemon curd sandwiches on white bread, with lashing of Stork® margarine cut into four. This may not sound much to some people, but to me it was a huge treat (we were never allowed white bread at home, let alone lemon curd!). To me, it was the way my grandmother and I communicated, it felt like 'our thing' and it made me feel close to her: I looked forward to it immensely. Looking back, I do remember, feeling a tinge of sadness we couldn't communicate more, especially when I saw my mother signing. To this day, I wish I could have had

141

more conversations with my grandmother, I loved her dearly, and I knew she loved me very much.

I found it easier to communicate with my grandfather. He always made a point of asking if I was okay, we would respond to each other by giving a smile and a thumbs-up gesture. Whenever I think about Grandpa, I recall him always smiling. I'm not sure if he always was but it is an emotional memory I treasure. My memories of his 'tailor room' are still etched into my mind - the iron, chalk markings, tailors table and the big mirror which we have in our house today. The flashing lights signalling visitors at the front door and his clients waiting patiently fascinated me as child. I proudly share with friends the fact my grandfather was a tailor. Grandpa was quite eccentric with a shock of long white hair and a beard to match. I'm sad my children never got to meet him; I know they would have loved him.

One of my fondest memories of both my grandparents was at my mother's 40th birthday party. They were dancing with each other next to the speaker, feeling the vibrations and having such a good time. Other great memories are of the Deaf Club Christmas Parties. We would play musical chairs and Grandpa would stand on the stage with his back to us. He would wave his white handkerchief and drop it , then we would rush and find a seat. I used to love these parties!

I have lost count of the number of times I have proudly shared with others that my mother is one of ten children and my grandparents were Deaf. My grandparents really were the 'glue' who held our family

Extended Family

together. I feel lucky to have grown up experiencing Deaf Culture.

It's these aspects of my family heritage which has made us all truly unique and have played a very important role in shaping the person I am today: for that I am very grateful.

Madeleine's Additional Reflections

Often when I am out with Dominique she will point out people signing. Within a blink I am off. It normally ends up I know what school they went to and the fact they knew my parents and many of my Deaf friends.

Madeleine With Sebastian And Dominique

Rachael and Michelle

Rachael and Michelle are my nieces. They have lived most of their young lives in Army quarters as their dad was in the Army.

I met with up with them, together - which was lovely. It is unusual to see the two together now as Rachael lives in Australia. It was a great opportunity to hear their thoughts and feelings about having Deaf grandparents. They recalled visiting about once a year due to the amount of moving around the army required.

Rachael and Michelle's Memories

Dad and Mum always tried to make sure we had a 'family visit' every year. We found the visit quite daunting. At home there was Mum, Dad and us, but when we visited them we were amongst this large family we did not see very often. We would have liked to have seen them more.

It was amazing for us when we did meet them all in Cambridge, we would thoroughly enjoy ourselves with our cousins, who were of similar ages. It was something different, but it was a little bit embarrassing for us as young children to be around grandparents whom we did not know very well, also they were Deaf.

Extended Family

When we wanted things like food and drink, we would go to Dad and ask him to ask for us. He wouldn't ask for us, oh no! He would show us how to ask for a drink of orange squash from Grandma and we would blush.

Grandpa was different, we would just look at him as he always had food in his beard (was he keeping it for later?). We would try and give him a kiss, which we were not too keen about, due to the food in his beard, but he would be really sweet and give us a kiss. The Hempstead family was always very 'kissy and huggy', even today when we meet up, it is kisses and hugs.

We loved, and got excited about, going to the Hempstead Annual Garden Party, at our grandparent's house, in Cambridge; it was the best place ever. Dad would be driving down the Avenue where they lived and we would get excited to see the house and Dad would drive into the gravel driveway (both Rachael and Michelle said, "We can hear the sound of the gravel now.") We would be at the most amazing house with the most amazing people. We have such fond memories, we would just look at everyone there, which was a mix of adults and children. My aunties and uncles were all hearing, but they would use Sign Language to chat to their parents who were both Deaf. We found we became more expressive, as it was such a natural thing to do!

We Are CODA

Deaf Stories

We Are CODA

*"You're so afraid that we'd look stupid.
Let them figure out how to deal with Deaf people.
We're not helpless."*

**Leo Rossi
from the film CODA**

Deaf Stories

As a CODA, I have found we gain the trust of Deaf people in a unique way. My siblings and I have been asked to interpret or communicate many times. This allows us to see the unfairness and discrimination they are subject to. Deaf people sometimes feel comfortable enough to share their current and past life experiences with a CODA more than a hearing person or even another Deaf person. A qualified interpreter must strictly interpret information provided and have guidelines to adhere to whereas a CODA who can communicate fluently has more leeway to add tone and sensitivity.

The following are true stories from Deaf people, which I have collected over the years. I kept most of these stories on scraps of paper (as is my habit) and put them in a suitcase. Now, it is time to let them see the light. Due to the sensitivity of these stories, names, places and dates have been changed.

Authorities Know Best

There are many situations where the authorities have assumed control of a Deaf person life and removed their choices. This was particularly prominent before the Second World War but has continued. It is my hope these stories would not happen today.

Baby Gone

In the mid 1930s, Jane, just 17, had 'gone' with a hearing boy not knowing what could happen. Jane was a young Deaf girl who did not know anything about sex or boys. Her real mother died when she was born while her father was away at sea. When he came home and was informed his wife had died giving birth to his Deaf daughter, he said he didn't want her and gave her to his next-door neighbour.

From that day Jane lived with the neighbour and her son. Jane's adoptive mother never signed or showed much affection to her. For many years Jane did not know the story of her birth; she always thought the neighbour was her real mother.

When Jane's adoptive mother found out Jane was pregnant, she was very angry and contacted the local Missionary for the Deaf. All Missionaries for the Deaf at the time were hearing. The missionary came to the house and told Jane as she was Deaf, young and unmarried, she could not keep the baby. Jane told me she was happy to have a baby of her own and did not see being Deaf and unmarried as a problem. She had knitted clothes for her baby and got everything ready. She had a boy and when she bought him home from the hospital, she breast fed him and loved him very much.

Without her knowledge, there had been a discussion about what would happen once the baby was born. The Missionary for the Deaf and Jane's adoptive mother decided the baby would be taken away.

Jane cried when she told me how it happened. Her aunt came to see her one day and asked if she could take the baby out for walk in the pram, he was still a small baby. Jane did not mind; she trusted her aunt with him.

After a while, Jane knew it was time for the baby's feed and waited by the window to look out for her aunt to come back with the baby. Jane kept looking and waiting and started to get very worried. Jane signed to her mother, *"Worried, where baby, not back, what happened."* Her mother very coldly said, *"Baby gone."* and that was that. Jane asked the Missionary for the Deaf, where her baby was. He told her, *"Not to worry."* Jane never found out happened to her son.

Too Sad To Sign

I remember Beth very well from my childhood. She was a plain looking person who would just sit at the Deaf Club and not sign. I signed to Mummy, *"Beth, wrong what? Sign never, sad."* So Mummy told me her story.

In the late 1940s, Beth found out that she was pregnant, she was very young. Beth was Deaf with learning difficulties and knew nothing about sex or the possibility of becoming pregnant. She was labelled 'an unmarried mother' and was hidden away during her pregnancy.

Mummy told me the Missionary for the Deaf, along with Beth's parents, decided she would not be allowed to keep her baby; that Beth was unfit to be a mother. The poor girl never saw the baby as it was taken at birth, (I do not know if it was a boy or a girl). Beth never got married and lived at home with her parents until they died. Then she moved into supported living.

Sometimes I wonder if she sat at the Deaf Club, not signing or joining the games, was not because she had a learning difficulty but because she was grieving for her lost baby!

Residential Deaf School Stories

In the past, many Deaf children were sent to Residential Schools for the Deaf at a very young age. Can you imagine, you are a hearing parent, with a child who was born Deaf and for this they would be taken away from you by the authorities?

A Welfare Officer would visit you at home to inform you that your Deaf child (usually 2 or 3 years old) would be taken away from you and you would only see them at the end of each term, which is about once every three months. Your child would live in a Residential Deaf school, sleep in a dormitory with other Deaf children who they didn't know and looked after by adults they had never met. This was the time when the authorities always knew best!

Many hearing parents believed the Welfare Officer knew what was best for their Deaf child, a child they could not communicate with. Some parents felt relieved as they did not know what to do. A parent and a child with completely different forms of communication, could be emotionally painful for the whole family.

No One To Tell

Paula was about two years old when she was taken away from her hearing parents and put into a residential school. At this young age she was at school full time and only saw her parents every three months. She says she was potty trained and weaned onto solids by staff at the school. Paula stayed at the school until she was sixteen years of age. These were not happy years for her.

Her relationship with her family deteriorated beyond repair. Going home to see them was miserable. At the end of each visit, she could not wait to get back to school, so she could communicate with her Deaf friends.

Paula made lifelong friends at school but always had a strained relationship with her parents. The removal from home caused a breakdown in communication and destruction of a loving relationship with her parents. Due to this, she was unable to tell them she had suffered physical abuse from the staff at the school. Paula also told me she was sexually abused too. At the time, she had no one to tell!

The Oral Way

John attended a Residential School for the Deaf and was fitted with hearing aids which were heavy and uncomfortable (nothing like the hearing aids fitted today). These were metal and did not fit properly. The hearing aid battery was strapped to the body. These hearing aids were transistorised and were known as 'Radionic Hearing Aids'.

John said, *"We would have to sit in a half circle strapped with these heavy hearing aids and machines trying to follow the audiologist lip pattern of sound. In the end, some of us would give up and try and communicate with each other in a different way. It was so difficult to try and follow a lip pattern, trying to see the difference between the words 'bath and path'. I got the lip pattern and sound wrong so often I would get hit by the teachers."*

Officially, he was not allowed to use Sign Language, as he was at an Oral Deaf School. *"Signing was something we created ourselves until I left school and joined the Deaf Community,"* he said. Even today he does not lip-read, he is happy signing.

Unacceptable Behaviour Explained

Barbara, a young Deaf girl with learning difficulties, was thirteen when she arrived at a Residential school for the Deaf. On her first evening in residence, Barbara behaved inappropriately, she pulled up her skirt and pulled down her knickers. The house staff explained to her through basic British Sign Language, this was not acceptable.

This was the first time anyone had been able to communicate to her through signing. The next day one of the house staff contacted Barbara's previous hearing school, which she had attended since she was four, to ask them questions about Barbara and her behaviour. The school stated she did it all the time and they would just say, *"No"*. They never explained to her what she was doing was not 'acceptable'. The staff at her previous school did not try to communicate with her so she could understand.

After it had been explained to her this behaviour was unacceptable by her new school, she never behaved in this way again.

Just A Number

A friend, Mike, started at a Residential School for Deaf children, when he was about five years old. The school's policy was to give all new children at the school a number on their first day. This meant their names were not used. Mike said all their clothes had labels sewn into them with their number on them instead.

When Mike went home at the end of term and his parents signed his name in their conversation, Mike told them he didn't have a name anymore, he was known by a number at school. When he got back to school, he was called his name again. He thinks his parents had something to do with it. Mike said he was a lot happier at school after this.

Government Property

Frances is a Deaf woman born to hearing parents. She told me, *"When born Government own me, they do what they want with me. Mum, Dad hearing, thought best what professionals tell them."*

Frances grew up believing she was owned by the government. They decided she should be taken away from her parents to go to a Residential School for the Deaf. She was abused there. The government had told her where to go and what to do and what was going to happen to her, but they never mentioned the abuse. Consequently, she thought being abused was normal.

It was only when she left school and spoke to other Deaf children, she realised it wasn't.

Even in her fifties she still believed the Government owned her. Frances has never married or had children. She says she does not feel she fits into the Deaf Community or to the hearing. She spends a lot of time on her own.

The Town with No Name

When I was a Residential Manager at a Deaf School, one of my duties at the beginning of the new school year was to meet all the new pupils. I remember one boy particularly well, David. David was thirteen years old and had been attending a hearing school. This was the first time he had been in a Deaf environment and at a school for Deaf children.

When I met him, I could see that he was 'blown away', by the expression on his face. His eyes and his mouth were wide open: I could see that he was loving the new surroundings and experience.

To get to know the children and make them feel more relaxed on their first day, I always asked them basic questions. I asked him his name and where he lived. He fingerspelled his name and signed the letter, *"H"* for where he lived. I looked at him looking questioningly and signed, *"H?"* he shrugged his shoulders and signed, *"H"* again. It was clear to me that he did not know the name of the town where he lived. We went to my office and I looked at his notes. I saw he was from Hartlepool. I fingerspelled the name of the town where he was from. Within minutes, David fingerspelled Hartlepool.

Now he knew the name of his home town: to see the smile on his face was a joy. From that day on he became confident and happy. David made many friends, most of whom have become long life friends.

Had to Choose

Randolf told me he remember feeling miserable when he came home at weekends from his Residential School for the Deaf. He loved being at school with his friends. For years, he would pretend to be happy at home. Christmas time was the worst: everyone opening presents, grandparents arriving, all sitting around the table, eating and chatting way. Randolf would just sit there and smile as his relatives would either over emphasise their movement of their mouths or over exaggerate gestures. Randolf loved his parents but just wished they would try and learn to sign and communicate with him in his language. After his years at school, and being with the Deaf Community, he decided to leave his hearing family and make the Deaf Community his family. It was a very hard decision to make but he knew if he lived within the hearing world, he would become depressed, more frustrated and live a miserable life.

How much better it would have been for Randolf if there had been mobile phones, computers, face time, and social media?

Audiology Assessment

The following story is a strange but funny story which happened many years ago. Would it happen today? I hope not!

Deaf parents had received funding for both of their boys to attend a Residential School for Deaf children. When children first arrive at a Deaf school, they have an appointment with an audiologist to access their hearing ability. Sometimes, it can take few days for the nurse and audiologist to see all the new children.

After the first few days, it was the boys turn to have their medical and hearing assessments. First, they saw the nurse and she gave them a clean bill of health. Then went to see the audiologist, who checked their hearing for hearing aids or any other language or hearing support. Suddenly, there was panic! The audiology assessment revealed one of the boys was hearing and he had to go home. What a shock it must have been for the whole family, and I wonder how it affected both boys, Deaf and hearing!

Left by the Bus Stop

In the 1950s, when Albert was seven years old, he was sent to a residential Deaf school. He was normally picked up at the end of term by his hearing parents at an arranged pick-up point, the local bus stop.

On this particular day, he was dropped off by a school friend and his parents. He waited with his friend and his friend's Deaf family. They waited and waited, but no one arrived to pick him up. He didn't know at the time but his parents did not want him anymore and just decided not to pick him up.

Luckily, his friend's parents took him home with them and where he ended up living and became one of their family. This was a time before Social Services and Child Protection would have got involved, and for him was a blessing. He had a wonderful childhood - he was very happy and well loved.

When he told us this story, he recalled how scared and confused he felt waiting at the bus stop, my heart just broke for him. It was cruel for his parents to abandon their child because he was Deaf.

What Accent?

A friend of mine, who was a Residential Manager at a Deaf School, told me this story. Part of his role was to visit each residential house in the evening. On one of his regular visits to the older girls' house, he said they were sitting around the TV watching their favourite Australian Soap, Neighbours: the girls loved it. At this time subtitles were not widely available, which meant the girls always had to ask questions about what was happening. Most of the programme was easy for the girls, Kylie Minogue and Jason Donovan and young romance. As the girls and him chatted away after the programme ended, one of the girls signed to him, *"Where England film Neighbours always hot weather?"* He explained Neighbours was not filmed in England, but in Australia. It was an Australian programme and they spoke with an Australian accent! This was quite a shock to them and opened up more questions about accents.

Lack of Information

The following stories show how Deaf people, from childhood, were not informed of information which was critical to their emotional health. Whether the information was withheld due to lack of thought, cruelty or a general misunderstanding of how to communicate with a Deaf person is anyone's guess!

Father's Funeral

Reginald still feels upset when he signs the story about when his father died. He was eleven years old and a pupil at a Residential School for the Deaf. Normally he would go home at the end of term. Many schools used to have 'termly boarders' which meant they went home at the end of term. Many children stayed at school during half-term.

Reginald was looking forward to going home to see his parents. He had a good relationship with his parents, especially his father. Children would be picked up on the last day of term by their parents or a relative.

When it came for Reginald to be picked up from school, a member of staff said he could not go home and had to stay another week with a member of staff. This did happen sometimes, in cases of emergency. No one told Reginald why he couldn't go home, he became worried and upset and wondered what was wrong.

At the end of the following week, Reginald was picked up to go home by a relative. When he got home, he signed to his mother, *"Stay school, why?"* His mother did not sign, so she gestured, *"Daddy dead, funeral."* Sixty years later, Reginald still can't understand why no one told him. He was not comforted, no one at school said anything and it continues to affect him.

Hereditary Hearing Loss

I was walking along the beach in Kent, having a peaceful time, just me! Since I have moved to the Kent coast, walking on the beach has been part of my routine, regardless of the weather. I even swim in the sea, the colder the better.

On this specific day, I went past a group of four people sitting on deckchairs, outside their beach hut (I would love a beach hut). Out of the corner of my eye I saw the young man in the group signing. He must have been about 25 years old. I stopped and double backed, to sign hello to them and then I started signing to the young man.

His face showed how happy he was to have someone sign to him. After a few minutes, I realised his communication was limited. What I mean by this is he was unable to respond fluently in Sign Language and would sometimes repeat himself or just nod, *"Yes."* This indicated to me that he did not fully understand what I was signing. So, I started to change my fluent signing to more basic signs with limited fingerspelling.

This is the same for hearing people, if you meet someone who has limited understanding of what you are saying, then you adapt accordingly.

As I am fluent in British Sign Language, it was easy for me to adapt my way of communicating by signing slowly and using lip pattern. This helped and we were then able to have a basic conversation, more along the lines of, *"School where? Live where? Have family?"*

He signed back to me, *"Me school hearing in unit, children disabled, London."* In English it would be, *"I attended school in London, it had a unit for Deaf children and children with disabilities."*

The three people with him were his mother, his sister and her husband. None of them could sign so they communicated mostly with gestures. When his sister introduced me to their mother I said, *"Hello, how are you, do you live here?"* She just smiled and did not say anything. His sister said their mother was hard-of-hearing and their grandmother had been Deaf.

I signed to the young man, *"Oh, mother hard-of-hearing and grandmother Deaf."* His look said it all, he had not known this! Then I thought oh dear, he didn't know. I asked his sister had anyone told him about his mother and grandmother. This was getting far away from what I hoped was going to be, *"Nice to meet a new Deaf person"* to *"Damn! I have created a situation."*

This was awkward for me and confusing for him. His sister asked me if I would sign for her and tell him the story about his mother and grandmother. I did not really want to be involved and felt very uncomfortable about being asked, but I agreed.

I felt so sad for the young man that he had missed out on having a better relationship with his mother and grandmother.

Why hadn't he been told? Did they not think it important or relevant? Or, did they assume he already knew? It made me feel angry with his family, and I wanted to ask them why? The poor, young, Deaf man. For years did not know his Deafness was most likely hereditary! Next time I am on the beach and see an unknown person signing, perhaps I should carry on walking. Knowing me, I know I won't!

Help! Where Are You Taking Me?

Victor, a young Deaf boy, was collected from his residential school on a Friday, as normal, by school transport to go home. He sat in the back of the car, looking out the window, and started to realise he was not on the same route home. Panic set in. He started banging on the window, pushing the driver's seat. The driver stopped the car and with the escort (all children picked up by taxis had to have an escort with them) tried to calm him down.

Neither the driver or the escort could sign or communicate with Victor. He thought he was being kidnapped. The taxi driver set off again, ignoring the boy sobbing in the back seat. Eventually, the taxi stopped at a house Victor had not seen before; he didn't know where he was or why he was there. He was still crying when he got out of the car. When he saw his mother, he hugged her so hard. His hearing parents had moved house without informing him; the school didn't tell him either.

Deaf Stories

Only Deaf At School

Neil was small for his age and wasn't a very popular at school but he said he loved residence, most of the children do, as it is where they make lifelong friends.

Neil had been a pupil at a Residential Deaf school since he was nine years old. Day children could start school from the age three. He had been happy at school, and was very excited about leaving and going out to work. Now 16, we had a chat about him and what his options were. There was an opportunity for him to go to College with the support of a Communication Support Worker (CSW) or having Communication Support at work. He could receive funding for the right job.

As we were signing away about his future possibilities, he said not to worry as he had decided what he wanted to do: to join the army.

"Oh, okay. Do the Army recruit Deaf people?" I asked. He smiled and was very cheery and said, *"It is not a problem."* I thought to myself, *'Why isn't this going to be an issue?'*

Then he said he was only Deaf when he was at a Deaf School, and when he left school, he would become hearing and join the Army.

I was so upset for him. How was I going to explain to him, he is Deaf, was born Deaf and this is why he was at a Deaf school? I thought it best for both of us if we sat down, had a drink and a burger to talk about his future. We sat down and chatted about him being Deaf and when he became Deaf and why he was at a Deaf school. He said he was happy being Deaf while he was at a Deaf school, but he insisted when he left, he will be hearing like his family. He started telling me about his family. All his family was hearing, they did not talk to him or sign to him about leaving school at sixteen. He had never met any Deaf people, adults or children, outside of school! He never fully understood he would be Deaf after leaving school.

Deaf Stories

Sex Abuse in the Deaf World

Sadly, I have been told about sex abuse by many Deaf people. It seems as if experiencing sexual abuse was commonplace for those in the Deaf community, hidden away within institutions. Only now is the vastness of the issue beginning to come to light. Unfortunately, I do not think the majority of past cases will ever be dealt with sufficiently.

Loss of a Friend

A dear friend told me this story. She and a Deaf friend spent a lot of good times together. They would go out to Deaf clubs and pubs to chat. During one of their chats, it was revealed the Deaf friend had been sexually abused as a child at a Residential Deaf school. She told it in a matter-of-fact way - it seemed she believed it was an 'okay' thing to have happened!

After they had talked further on the subject, the Deaf friend said she would tell the police as long as her hearing friend was her communication support. Of course, the hearing friend agreed.

They went to the police station. The police thought it would be better, due to the nature of the issue, for them to go to a safe house with two police officers, one who was female.

As they sat down the Deaf friend told her story about what happened to her. Then her story of her abuse started to change. She started talking about how as she was abused, she felt she could abuse other children at the school. Her hearing friend began to feel shaky as she communicated this to the police as the story started to change from being sexually abused to sexually abusing others. She felt she could no longer communicate on behalf of her Deaf friend. The conversation was stopped and the hearing friend was asked to leave immediately by the police. Her Deaf friend looked confused and upset.

Since that day they have never seen each other so the hearing friend does not know the outcome.

Alleged Sex Abuse at a Deaf Residential School

Joanne attended a Catholic Residential School for Deaf children, from a young age. She was a boarder at the school and would go home at the end of each term.

As it was a Catholic school, all children had to attend mass and go to confessions with a priest and usually took their First Holy Communion by the time they were seven or eight years old.

Before Catholics receive their First Holy Communion, according to the Catechism of the Catholic Church, each person must receive the 'Sacrament of Confession'. The Sacrament of Confession is a form of training

Deaf Stories

for preparation, rather than a cleansing of the soul. Confessions after the First Holy Communion bring reconciliation between God and the penitent (feeling or showing sorrow).

In this school, the children would go to Confession and tell their sins in what is known as a 'confessional box' based at the church. With Deaf children, it was different. Joanne signed, *"Told write down sins on paper. Sins what! I was a child, did not do sins."* Yet, she always had to do Penance. The priest would write the penance on the same paper. Penance is a 'remission of sin' which is given based on repentance and confession.

Joanne like the other children would go into the confessional box with the priest with her piece of paper saying, *"No sins."* but she was always given Penance. Joanne's Penance was to sit on the priest lap, undo her blouse and show him her breasts, then he would give her Penance which was always three Hail Marys. Joanne said this carried on for a few years from when she was about twelve. Nothing was ever mentioned or told to anyone. Even in her seventies, Joanne talks about it as if it was just one of those things which happen in life.

Put Your Hands Up!

Janet, a Deaf lady, was giving a presentation on 'Deaf Children and Abuse' to a mixed Deaf and hearing group at a conference. She was concerned as because it was a mixed group of Deaf and hearing and she did not know what their responses would be. Luckily, an interpreter had been booked for her.

Janet very bravely started her presentation by asking the hearing participants to raise their hands if any of them had been sexually abused as a child, or if they knew of a child who had been. She waited for a few moments: not one hearing participant put up their hand. She thought this might happen; it is a lot to ask someone in a group setting.

Janet then asked the same question to the Deaf participants. Within seconds, every Deaf participant had put their hand up.

When I relayed this story to a hearing friend, she said, *"Well, maybe it had happened to one or more of the hearing participants, but they did not want to say anything."*

Do Deaf people admit the abuse they have suffered more than hearing people because they are more open or is it because Deaf people think that being abused as a child is normal? This took place was about 40 years ago. I wonder what the responses would be today.

Just a Telling-off!

This story came to the attention of the Deaf Community was when the police took this man to the Welfare Officer for the Deaf.

Paul, a Deaf man from the Deaf Community, was known to be a homosexual at the time when homosexuality was illegal. It was always known that he was gay, but as far as the Deaf Community were concerned, it didn't matter to them.

Paul was inappropriately approaching a school boy on a bus. The bus conductor phoned the police and reported that he had seen Paul approach the boy and had upset him. These were the days when all buses had one bus driver and a conductor who collected the

Deaf Stories

fares, helped people on and off the bus, and rang the bell to let the driver know when to stop and start the bus.

When the police came, they tried to talk to Paul. When they realised he was Deaf, they did not take him to the police station, but to the Welfare Officer for the Deaf.

At the time, the Welfare Officer was also the interpreter, unqualified but could sign well. The police left it up to the Welfare Officer to deal with the situation. All he got was a 'telling off' by the Welfare Officer, and a, *"Don't do it again."* I would have thought the man should have been questioned at the police station as he was accused of approaching young boy for sexual reasons. I wonder if a hearing gay man would have been treated so leniently!

Institutional Miscommunication

There are many serious stories I have been told which could have more positive beginnings (or endings) if there was greater awareness and better sharing of information in institutions such as banks, prisons, schools, hospitals and across all social services and within society in general.

A Prison Headache

Sam, a Deaf man, also had learning difficulties. He was convicted of a crime and sent to prison for a few months. Sam was very scared in prison. He didn't know what was going to happen to him and really could not understand why he was there.

One day he tried to explain to one of the prison officers that he needed to see a doctor as he had a bad headache. Luckily, he had been able to get the prison officer to understand what he was trying to say. The next day he had his appointment with the prison doctor.

The doctor understood Sam had a headache, but as the doctor had not looked at Sam's medical report (it had not arrived at the prison yet) the doctor offered Sam medication. Sam panicked. Due to lack of communication support, he could not explain to the doctor he had an allergy to the medication. Sam started gesturing to try to tell the doctor he couldn't take the medication. The doctor misunderstood and pressed the panic button. Two prison officers came in, jumped on Sam, held him down and then took him back to his cell. Eventually, the doctor realised why Sam panicked and thank goodness it didn't happen again. With proper communication procedures in place this would not have happened.

Hospital Treatment

A friend texted me to let me know an elderly Deaf friend, Iris, was in a local hospital. Iris was a friend of my mother; they had been at school together. I visited her the same day and was shocked to see Iris laying there looking so tiny and frail. It was upsetting to see her in such a state, but upset soon changed to anger. I tapped her on the shoulder, and when she turned to look at me, she cried.

Iris tried to sign to me through her tears. I was signing, *"Wrong what?"* After a minute or so, she pointed to her mouth, shook her head. I realised she was hungry and maybe thirsty. When I checked the medical board at the end of her bed, there was nothing written down saying 'Deaf patient'. I was mad. I kept calm and signed to Iris, *"I shall find staff, don't worry back soon."* I very calmly (well trying to stay calm) went down the corridor to find a member of the nursing staff. When I asked if they knew Iris was Deaf, *"Umm, no."* was the reply.

By this time, I was fuming, poor Iris. It turned out she had not had anything to eat or drink all day. The ward staff apologised profusely they thought she was ignoring them. To me, it was beside the point, she still should have had some attention. When I left in the evening, Iris had something to eat and drink, the staff had some Deaf Awareness, and 'Deaf Patient' was put on her medical chart. Leaving Iris in better hands made her feel so much better, we had a hug and I promised to visit her again soon.

Iris passed away not long after, but at least it was from natural causes.

Teacher Training

In the early 2000s, I interviewed a Deaf person for a volunteering position with children. She so much wanted to be a Teacher for the Deaf since she was a young girl, but when she applied for teacher-training, she was informed she was not suitable!

She was very upset and didn't understand why. When she asked questions and investigated why she had been rejected she was told she had not been suitable because she was 'Deaf without speech' and could not lip read. The teacher-training course could not accommodate her as all trainee teachers have to do their training in hearing schools! I asked another Deaf friend of mine (who is a teacher) is this true? She said yes. She did have some voice and could lip-read so she was accepted on the teacher-training programme.

Employment Support

Discrimination against Deaf people in employment is still happening. This is a text conversation between me and a Deaf friend regarding him needing support in the way of a Communicator for training. I knew Peter through supporting him in other situations prior to this event. The text messages between us is word for word, nothing has been added or changed (except the names). Please remember Deaf writing is often done in short sentences and phrases.

> **Peter:** *Hello! Are you available on 13. and 14. February for training induction - I need BSL service...? I can pay you for this... Peter.*

> **Me:** *Hi Peter, Where is the induction? How much for the day? Madeleine*

> **Peter:** *from 7.30 to 16.00 on 13. February on 14 February for training induction. For delivery driver by (company name)*

> **Me:** *How much money to pay me for both days. Where is the training?*

> **Peter:** *It is up to you. I think I get ATW funding for you, Ok? (included was the address) Hello! What do you think about this? (My note - ATW = Access to Work)*

> **Me:** *I am at work will text later today.*

> *Then he sent me this from the company who had offered him the post of a delivery driver.*

> **Peter:** *However, I'm afraid we will have to put your application on hold until we have followed the correct procedure which should have been done prior to me giving you the job offer, and I sincerely apologise that this was not done before.*

> *Please do not come in on 13th February 2023. Due to the medical information you have*

declared, as a duty of care to yourself we would like to do an occupational health referral through (xxxxxxx).

Please read and fill in all relevant information on the attached form below.

You will then receive an email from (xxxxxxx) asking you to complete an online medical questionnaire, that is where you must tell (xxxxxxx) about the medicals you have mentioned. Medicals?

I did not know being Deaf was a medical 'situation'! It appears nothing much has changed over the years regarding having access to an interpreter for work situations. One would have thought with all the media covering the related issues, British Sign Language rallies and Government discussions to have British Sign Language recognised and accepted as a language in its own right, a difference would have been seen and a change made!

When is BSL going to be recognised as a language?!

One Deaf acquaintance was looking for a book on painting and went into a well-known high street bookshop. As she was looking around, she saw that the staff had put British Sign Language books under Mental Health Section. It made her so angry.

She took the shop assistant to the Mental Health book section and wrote down on a piece of paper, *"Why put British Sign Language under Mental Health? British Sign Language is a language, should be under the language section."* The shop assistant apologised took all the Sign Language books out and put them in the Language Section, while my friend watched. Deaf people have spent many years, campaigning, fighting for their language rights and this still happens.

Unable to Cope

A Deaf partner of a dear Deaf friend had given birth to a severely disabled baby. It was a great shock to them both. The mother tried to cope with the situation but just couldn't and left, leaving her partner with the baby.

Social workers, health visitors and other supportive agencies visited my friend and his baby at their home. He tried his best but was traumatised and could not manage. He was depressed and frustrated. All he wanted was the support with interpreters present, but he only got an interpreter occasionally. He felt isolated and did not know what to do.

In the end, after trying so hard for so long, he had a breakdown and ended up in an awful situation and was sent to a Mental Health Unit for Deaf people.

Farm Boy

I was told of a Deaf boy with hearing parents who were farmers. He never went to school and didn't even know school existed. When he was five years old, his parents sold him to another local farmer. The child worked at the farm without pay until he was thirty years old. Eventually, someone told the police, who then contacted a social worker who started to ask questions and he was rescued. I do not know if anyone was prosecuted.

If Only He Had Communicated With Someone!

Robert was a very funny, but quiet, young Deaf man. He had a wicked sense of humour and was a great artist. I wish I had kept the little drawings he did of me.

Robert attended a Residential School for the Deaf until he was sixteen years old. He was happy at school, he did not have many close friends, but fitted in well with the other children in the residential house he stayed in. He made it obvious to some of the other children at school, he was not happy at home as his parents were hearing, very busy and worked very hard. Robert was an only child.

When Robert left school, he decided not to go on to college, so he went back to live at home. It took him a while to find a job, but eventually he found a job he liked and started to work full time. As he was earning money, he went to the bank to get a loan to buy a new moped, which would help him get him to work and back.

Robert was able to pay the loan from the bank, using his wages until he was put on reduced hours at work. No one is quite sure why he decided to get a bank loan in the first place when he could have asked his parents for the money.

Robert began receiving letters from the bank demanding payments and threatening him with court, and at the same time, the interest on the loan was increasing. Due to British Sign Language being his first language, Robert's understanding of written English was limited. To try and understand a professional letter would have been very difficult for him.

Sadly, Robert didn't discuss this issue with his parents and kept ignoring the letters. Robert hung himself and his parents found his body. They were devastated and could not understand why he would commit suicide. He had Deaf friends he could have spoken to. It has been over thirty years since Robert passed away. He was only twenty and had so much potential.

On The Radio

This story is about Deaf parents who only had one child, who was hearing. They were unsure how to teach him to speak, so they came up with the idea of putting the radio on all day, every day, for their child to listen and learn how to speak English. One day they invited their hearing neighbours over to show how proud they were of their child who had learnt how to speak English via the radio.

The neighbours listened to their child and the Deaf parents suddenly started to feel worried. Why had their neighbours used the 'confused' facial expression. The neighbours tried to explain the child was not speaking English, but French. The Deaf parents had not realised their child was listening to a French speaking programme!

We Are CODA

My CODA Life

"*I get to be their voice, and I mean that very literally. It always was and is a very proud feeling when I could take something complex and translate it into something very clear, and understandable... Deaf people are capable of anything and everything. Deaf people are just that; they're people.*"

Austin Johnson
in the interview, *Hearing like Me,*
with Ashley McGoey

Education and Employment

This chapter touches on schools and educational facilities for Deaf people. Within it I recall my experiences working in the Education sector and as an Advocate for Deaf people. I fully credit my background as a CODA for enabling me to be involved in this way.

Mary Hare Grammar School

Mary Hare School was established by Mary Adelaide Hare in 1916. It was initially known as Dene Hollow Oral School for the Deaf. In commemoration of its Founder, it was renamed Mary Hare Grammar School in 1946. The school today is the largest school for Deaf Children in the UK, but is no longer classed as a Grammar School (which I think is a shame as it was the only grammar school for Deaf children). The school today still provides boarding and day schooling for children from Reception to Year 13 (aged 4-19).

Communication at the school surrounds the English Language, both spoken and written, British Sign Language is not used in regular classes. The pupils learn by using voice and the use of English, without the use of British Sign Language. Nowadays, they do offer students the opportunity to gain a Level 2 qualification in BSL with a view to review as a possible Key Stage 4 option (A-Level) in the future.

Universities

There isn't a university for Deaf students in the UK. (Universities have always been a problem for Deaf people who use BSL as their main form of Communication). There are currently five universities which offer undergraduate Deaf studies, which include interpreter training and study the history of manualist/oralist debate. These universities offer support for Deaf students using variety of forms of communication. There are a few other universities which offer postgraduate courses for Deaf Teacher Training.

Gallaudet University, USA

Situated in Washington DC, Gallaudet University is the world's only university for Deaf students where lectures and seminars are given using American Sign Language. The University was founded as a college in 1864 by Edward Gallaudet. The campus is set in ninety-nine acres of land. In 1988, students protested for a Deaf University President. After a week long campaign called. *Deaf President Now*, Dr. I. King Jordan became the first in the University's 124-year history.

In 2007, when staying in Washington DC, I spent a day at Gallaudet University. I thought, *'Wow! Here I am at this famous University.'* It was very exciting and I felt honoured to be there. Knowing I was going to visit Gallaudet I brushed up on my ASL fingerspelling and a few basic signs, hoping it would enable me to communicate better. It did help immensely and the students were very helpful and taught me a few more signs whilst I was with them.

BSL and ASL, are two completely different languages. In ASL the alphabet is signed with one hand whilst in BSL it is signed using both hands. Many people assume someone signing ASL and someone signing BSL would be able to easily communicate with one another. This is not necessarily the case.

My Employment

Much of my early employment as a Communication Support Worker (CSW) was at Cambridge Regional College. I used my teaching qualification here and taught British Sign Language a couple of evenings each week. My students were adults from many walks of life. At the time, you didn't officially need any qualifications to teach BSL or even to teach adults, but I felt I had suitable qualifications to do so with my teacher training, CODA background and BSL Level 3.

At this time, I also volunteered at the CDA and organised Deaf and hearing groups alongside Linda Fincham. At this group we played Deaf games and taught BSL Level 1 and 2. It was a popular group with over 50 members.

I was inspired to progress my career and applied to work at the Royal School for the Deaf, Derby. I knew I would be immersed in a strong Deaf environment. I felt confident I could do the job if only given the chance, after all, the children who I would be supporting were part of my Deaf community.

We Are CODA

Royal School for the Deaf, Derby

In 1995, I saw an advert for a Residential Manager at the Royal School for the Deaf, Derby. Still thinking I would not stand a chance, I applied and was invited for interview at the school. At my interview, I looked around the school, met the children and the staff, and to my surprise I was offered the post, beginning in September.

It was the toughest job I ever had; I loved and hated it.

Initially, some of the Deaf staff appeared to transmit the feeling of, '*Just because she can sign, she thinks she is Deaf*' and blanked me. I found this emotionally painful. However, their behaviour changed when they found out who my father was. The knowledge that I was, 'Hempstead Daughter' went around the school and Deaf staff. Some of the hugged me and suddenly I was more accepted. It was here I met my dear friend Janice Silo, who was one of the Deaf teachers. We are still good friends.

Similarly, the hearing staff believed the same as Deaf staff did, '*Just because she has Deaf parents and signs, she thinks she is Deaf.*' Unfortunately, during the five years I was in this role my relationship with most of the hearing staff did not improve.

As Residential Manager, I was always thinking of different ways to support the children who lived there. One idea was to have an international residential exchange. The school and parents agreed it could be wonderful for the children. So, I connected with a Dutch Deaf school. John, one of my Deaf staff, and I flew over to Holland for a few days to meet the teachers and the

Education and Employment

pupils to arrange the exchange. I introduced myself to the pupils explaining some of the rules and I signed in BSL, *"No naughty"*. The whole class gave me a strange look, the teacher asked me, *"What was the sign?"* I said the sign for naughty, he smiled, *"Here it is the sign for Gay."* We did all giggle later about it!

The exchange went ahead and was a great success for the children. Unfortunately, I believe, the exchange process was not utilised to its full potential. When the Dutch Deaf school came over for the reciprocal visit, they were unable to take part in the working school day. We did socialise with them after school hours and the children continued to build their friendships, exchange different signs and exchange addresses. I wonder if any of them have kept in touch!

One of my duties was to interview new residential staff. It was an aspect I really enjoyed as I could have a large input into choosing the right staff for the children. One of the staff I employed was Nick Browne. He was an outstanding young Deaf Black man who had been to university. He was a good role model for the boys in residence. What I did not know at that time was that Nick was the first Deaf Black man to employed as Staff in Residence. Nick and I are still friends today and I am his hearing son's hearing Godmother.

Rangammal Memorial (Deaf) School, Tamil Nadu, India

While working at the Royal School for the Deaf, Derby, we had a visit from an Indian headmistress from a Deaf school in India. I saw it as an opportunity to make a visit to her school. I hunted her out while she was looking around the school to ask her if I could do a visit as a volunteer to the school, she said, "*Yes!*" I was so excited; I had been dreaming about going to India for years.

The following year I was off, taking pens and notebooks for the teachers. I spent three weeks of my school summer holidays there. The trip was an emotional journey; the children had never had anyone to visit them who could sign. The older children, with my support, learned BSL. I only knew three Tamil Signs, which didn't help much.

The children learned very quickly and visited a hearing school nearby to show how proud they were of signing their names and other basic signs. They taught me some Indian dancing as they were practising for a dancing competition and were making their own clothes for the show. I unpacked my large rucksack and gave them

Madeleine with some of the children at Rangammal School

Education and Employment

most of my clothes for them to adapt and use for the show.

When I left, some of the older children cried, as did I, it was hard for me to leave. It was an experience never to be forgotten.

After I left the school, with a lighter rucksack, I took the bus to Chennai, Tamil Nadu to visit another Deaf school, this one just for Girls. No signing was allowed, but we did a bit, secretly. I flew home, an exhausted but very happy traveller.

In 2000, I felt I couldn't progress further in this post. I wanted to empower all groups of minority groups, including Deaf people. To do this I needed to look further afield.

Home-Start Brent

In 2000, I left the Royal School for the Deaf, Derby and moved to Holloway (not the prison) London, to begin a new job. My new role was as Full-time Manager of Home-Start Brent: the office was in Harlesden. The purpose of the role was to train volunteers to support parents with at least one child under the age of five. It was similar to the Government initiative Sure Start, which had started around a similar time.

Initially, I found it a struggle as I didn't really know the area and was new to working in London. However, it was an exciting time as I began to look at how we could support Deaf families in the area. After some time, a Deaf mother was referred to the Home-Start programme. As I was the only person on our team who could sign, I took on this family case.

189

Once again, I discovered the Family Social Worker (FSW) allocated to the case had no idea how to work with a Deaf person. They had no training or any personal Deaf awareness. The Deaf mother was required to attend Family Court and unsurprisingly there was no interpreter for her (someone had forgotten to book one!). I was asked by the judge if I would interpret for him. I declined to do so as I was there as an advocate for Deaf mother and the only support she had. I felt my role as Advocate was to communicate with her so she had as much understanding of the situation (and potential outcomes) as possible. If I had agreed to take on the role of interpreter I would have been unable to adequately support her and ensure she had the opportunity to speak up for herself. I felt able to assist in this way as I had provided this type of support many times for my parents and their friends in the past: it is a significant part of CODA life.

Another time, I supported the same the Deaf mother at a supervised visit from the FSW. She asked the Deaf mother questions while she trying to feed her baby. To answer the questions, the mother had to stop feeding her baby and put the baby down, which ultimately led to the baby crying. I explained to the FSW, *"For the mother to 'bond with her child' she needs to feed her and requires her hands to be able to do so. She also needs her hands to talk."*

The Family Social Worker was very pleased I had explained this to her and she waited until the mother hands were free. If the mother had been on her own,

Education and Employment

without support and unable to respond to the FSW, she could have been written down as being uncooperative.

Whilst at Home-Start I was offered a chance to visit a new Disability Project, run by a group of wealthy companies, in Dhaka, Bangladesh. I was asked to look at the possibilities of starting an organisation similar to Home-Start. Of course, I said, "Yes," and flew out a few months later for a two-week visit. In Bangladesh there was little support for people with disability. When I asked about the support for Deaf people, I was told, *"There aren't any Deaf people, only blind."*

At the time the programme only considered people with obvious physical disabilities. People with more hidden disabilities, such as Deaf people, were not considered to need the support. It was a time when people who could not maintain a job were institutionalised, they were not valued.

Papworth Trust 2002-2003

I decided to move back to Cambridge to be nearer family. I secured the job as Director of Papworth Advocacy for Disabled People called 'Our Voice' funded by the Papworth Trust. They believed every disabled person had a right to have someone to support them to 'speak up' for themselves.

At the time there was on-site housing for people with disabilities. They had access to care staff, advocacy and a timetable of organised events and day trips. Within the Trust there was a mixture of people with a range of disability, including people who were Deaf, wheelchair users and learning difficulties.

My team included Deaf and hearing staff; we really were able to offer a full range of advocacy to all clients at Papworth Trust. It was a great job. Six months into this role, I was involved in a serious car crash. It took place on the dual carriageway between Baldock and Royston. I even had an ambulance with flashing blue lights take me to Stevenage Hospital.

This incident effected my ability to drive, work and look after myself for a long time. I tried to go back to my post as Director, first-of-all in a part-time capacity, hoping eventually to get back to full-time. Sadly, this was not possible. After a while, I agreed to resign from my post and concentrate on getting well. It took over three years before I was able to get back to even part-time work.

Education for Prisoners

You might wonder why I have brought this subject up in this book. Supporting Deaf prisoners has been part of my volunteering and working life for over twelve years.

My journey of supporting prisoners began after I watched the 1989 documentary *14 Days in May*. It is about prisoners on Death Row in the USA. After watching it, I became involved in a group who wrote to prisoners who were waiting to be executed.

A few years later, I read an article regarding Deaf prisoners in the UK who were serving a Double Sentence. Not only were Deaf prisoners doing time, but they were also isolated from the Deaf Community and had no or little communication using BSL.

Education and Employment

In 2000, the Birmingham Institute for the Deaf (BID) received government funding to set up the Deaf Prison Project (DPP). Volunteers and advocates were trained and vetted to work with Deaf prisoners in England. The project was funded for ten years.

During this time, I supported prisoners in fourteen prisons. I supported the prisoners in parole hearings, advocacy - by attending appointments within the prison, liaising with the prisoners' families, solicitors, social services and probation officers and I worked to ensure prisoners were supported after they were released.

Prisoners (particularly sex offenders) are required to attend training as part of their rehabilitation programme. Training was to include anger management, problem solving and relationship-management. This training however was not offered to Deaf prisoners. When prison staff knew a communicator would be needed (and thus paid for) it was always decided the Deaf prisoner did not need to attend any of the courses or training.

Deaf prisoners were worried and would ask me why they were unable to attend the training they had been informed was required for release. I always enquired for them but just got excuses, *"They don't have the time", "The prisoner does not need to attend."* Or, *"The course has been cancelled."* and so on.

Deaf prisoners not only missed out on these important sessions; they also missed out on classroom education as Communication Support Workers (CSW) were unavailable at the prison.

We Are CODA

It infuriated me as Deaf people, including prisoners, miss out time and time again due to lack of access to a CSW. Why was it never budgeted for? Each college which supplies education should have in their budget, costs for a CSW. To not provide this, breaches the Human Rights Commission's statement, 'No person shall be denied a right to education'.

I wrote an article in response to an Education Committee inquiry titled, *Are prisoners being left behind?* I never thought it would be published. Can you imagine how shocked I was when I received notification stating my submission had published it on the committee's website? I was pretty pleased with myself. There have been many published reports about Deaf prisoners. None mention how 'Education in Prison', is limited or, in some cases, non-existent for Deaf prisoners.

I am a bit of a 'worrier' when putting my real name out on the internet. Working in prisons for over twelve

The Team on the Prison Project, Birmingham 2000

years always made me feel the less my name is out on social media the better. Even when I was a Charity Trustee for Canterbury Diocesan Association For The Deaf, I asked the Charity Commission if my name could be withheld from public record: they agreed. Now, here I am writing a book (which I hope will be a best seller) with my real name. Scary!

British Sign Language, Teaching and Interpreting Qualifications

There is a lot of politics around who can or should be allowed to interpret and communicate on behalf of a Deaf person. In the UK, the leading awarding body, Signature, states you need to have achieved a BSL Level 6 qualification and have passed an interpreting course. After this you need to register with the professional body, National Registers of Communication Professionals working with Deaf and Deafblind People (NRCPD). In addition to this, interpreters need a DBS certificate and professional indemnity insurance.

To teach BSL at GCSE level current guidance suggests teachers should have at least a Level 4 BSL qualification and be working towards Level 6 by 2030. It is also suggested they should achieve Qualified Teacher Status (QTS). Again, to be fully in place by 2030. It is also preferred that teachers of BSL be Deaf and that long-term development should be geared towards Deaf predominance in this sector. There is no substitute for learners engaging directly with Deaf people as they study BSL and associated cultural topics.

In the UK, the process for achieving each level is very prescriptive, you have to go through every single BSL qualification even if you have signed your entire life and have a high level of BSL. This can be expensive. In Australia, through Australian Sign Language Interpreters' Association (ASLIA) the system works more fairly (in my opinion). If you are a CODA, ASLIA will assess your level of sign and put you straight in at an appropriate level.

As a hearing person, even as a CODA, I have experienced significant discrimination when trying to achieve my BSL qualifications. Some people, (hearing and Deaf) once they learn I am a CODA, often assume I only know family signs. For example, I went for an interview to attend a Level 4 Course in British Sign Language and met with an interpreter at the course centre. She asked me about my background. I started my reply with my parents were Deaf: big mistake! She looked at me in a negative way and said, *"Mmm, you only know family signs,"* and walked off. *'Here we go again!'* I thought and I walked out. Some Deaf people think BSL should be reserved for Deaf people.

I believe there should clearer guidance and more flexibility to who can teach BSL. I have known of hearing and Deaf people (with limited communication skill) receiving employment by Further Education establishments to teach Sign Language.

I asked a few Deaf people who used to teach British Sign Language in Further Education and others who taught Deaf people, their thoughts on who should teach Sign Language. They believe hearing people should not teach British Sign Language.

Education and Employment

I enquired whether they had Deaf parents. All of them said they had hearing parents. Then I asked, *"How did you find out about Deaf History, Culture and learn British Sign Language?"* Their answers were, we learnt as we went along from the Deaf Community. I also asked about their own teachers and where they went to school. They all said their teachers were hearing and they went to Deaf Residential Schools, which they loved and it was where they learned about their Deaf Identity.

My response to them was, I was brought up in the Deaf Community, thrived in Deaf Culture, learned about Deaf history and British Sign Language through my Deaf parents. Therefore my 'Deaf Identity' started when I was born, at my mother's knee, whereas they had to learn about their 'Deaf Identity' later in life.

Interestingly, most of the Deaf people I asked did not have a teaching qualification or have a high-level qualification in BSL. They admitted they got their teaching positions due to being Deaf. I do not mention this to detract from the fact they are amazing Sign Language tutors and highly professional in their work but to highlight the biases and discrimination around the Deaf Culture. I am highly-qualified in Sign Language and have worked as a tutor, however as a hearing person I might be seen as unacceptable by the Deaf Community. Deaf people sometimes feel it is a case of a hearing person taking a Deaf person's job, whether or not they are more qualified.

When I mentioned this to the Deaf tutors, they shrugged their shoulders and admitted I had a valid point. I do not think this is limited to Deaf Culture though: should an English person, who has a French Language Degree, speaks fluent French, lives in France and socialise within the French community, teach French? Would they be discriminated against because they not of French origin?

Deaf Action states that pitting hearing and Deaf people against each other, does not allow space for co-operation, nor does it respect the role hearing people can play in the Deaf Community. I personally feel some hearing people can be supportive within the Deaf community as long as they understand the cultural boundaries. Additionally, Deaf people need to share their feelings if they feel boundaries after overstepped to help a hearing person understand more. Greater cooperation between both worlds would be of great benefit.

To be or not to be... a qualified interpreter

Officially I have a BSL Level 6 qualification and hold a Teaching Qualification. I can therefore officially teach BSL up to the Level 3 qualification.

I chose not to pursue past Level 6; to become a trainee interpreter, and beyond, because of the political and social implications it may have on my life. What I mean by this is some Deaf people see an interpreter as separate from the Deaf community. I have a friend who picked up BSL later in life and has recently qualified as an interpreter. Since qualifying she has less social contact with Deaf people and their community.

I feel if I say I am interpreter to a new group of Deaf people as a hearing person, their attitude will change towards me. Deaf People are more accepting of me in a social situation without the qualification. My Deaf community is my life and extremely important to me. I do not need or want the interpreter status.

In my experience, a lot of CODAs end of up working alongside Deaf People without an interpreting qualification but have very strong BSL Skills.

In general, CODAs are not acknowledged much within the Deaf or hearing communities. CODA UK&Ireland are only just having their first conference this year (2024). CODA International, based in the USA is a little further forward and was officially founded in 1983.

I would encourage everyone to become more Deaf aware and learn Sign Language even at the lower levels, as you never know who you may meet, when it will come in 'handy' and you may gain a love of the language itself.

We Are CODA

A Bicultural and Bilingual World

Importance of CODAs

In general, CODAs are not acknowledged much within the Deaf or hearing communities. CODA UK & Ireland are only just having their first conference in 2024. CODA International, based in the USA is a little further forward and was officially founded in 1983.

In my experience, CODAs play a vital role in the Deaf community. We are bridges between the Deaf and hearing worlds. Growing up in a bicultural environment, they provide advocacy and support to their Deaf family members while fostering understanding between the two communities. Their unique perspective and experiences can contribute to the cultural richness and continuity of the Deaf community, helping to preserve Deaf heritage and promote inclusion.

My Bilingual and Bicultural Life in the Deaf and hearing Community

I always knew I came from a unique family, I did not realise how unique, until recently. It seems in the 'World of CODAs', we are the only family to have ten hearing children born to Deaf parents! I have not met another family like mine, and I have searched for a very long time.

Those who know me know I'm not keen on being labelled, nor do I particularly like the term CODA, however sometimes a label means one can be recognised and supported.

Finding Research

Trying to find anything which was written specifically on the Spoken Language, Sign Language, Community, and bilingualism of a CODA has not been easy. However, after a lot of searching I came across a very detailed and supportive research paper I felt was relevant to my story. What a find! On discovery, I felt excited about it and wondered what the differences would be, if any! Families are all different, but I still feel that CODAs have something in common due to their bilingual and bicultural lives.

The research, *Hearing Children of Deaf Parents: Gender and Birth Order in the delegation of the interpreter role in culturally Deaf families* (Moroe & de Andrade, 2018) and was conducted with CODAs from Gauteng, an urban and economically active province in South Africa. Maybe one day I shall visit CODAs living there!

In this chapter, I have taken key statements from the article, which I feel are relevant to me, and have reflected upon them and how they relate to my own experiences.

Globally, it is suggested that 90% of people with audiological deafness who have children have hearing children (Christodoulou et al. 2009).

This is still true in 2024. Surprisingly, many people think Deaf parents do not have hearing children.

International studies conducted on hearing children of Deaf parents show that these children are raised in families where there appears to be unique dynamics in relation to hearing children born to hearing parents. Authors such as Preston (1995) report that hearing children of Deaf parents are raised in unique, extraordinary family settings… the lives of hearing children of Deaf adults (CODAs) may inherently incorporate the ambiguity of being culturally 'Deaf' and yet functionally hearing.

I agreed with this statement; we could be viewed as culturally Deaf as we often use sign language to communicate even though my siblings and I are 'functionally hearing'. The difference here adding to the 'culturally deaf' element is our chosen form of communication even when no Deaf person is around. On British Sign Language Week in 2024, my five sisters and I got together and signed to honour the occasion.

Hearing people who identify with Deaf culture, such as hearing children of Deaf parents, may also form part of the Deaf community. Because of such diversity within the community, in order for one to enter the Deaf community, 'one must adopt a cultural view of Deafness and be

> *proficient in Sign Language' (Singleton and Tittle 2000:222).*

This is partly true; it is not all about Sign Language. It is essential as a CODA to respect where we stand within the Deaf Culture and Community and carefully consider the cultural appropriateness of our actions. For example, it is not up to a CODA (or any hearing person) to create a new sign or tell a Deaf person their 'Sign' is wrong and the CODA is right.

> *Deaf people would not be regarded as disabled if they were given access to information and the means to communicate with the hearing community (Napier 2002).*

Deaf people all over the world and for hundreds of years have always wanted 'Equal Access' to information and rights! They are still fighting for it today. Things are changing, but very slowly which is disappointing. One example of a positive step is the UK Government recognised British Sign Language as a language on March 18th 2003. However, Deaf children are unable to have a GSCE qualification in their own language - this is an issue which is currently being talked about within the UK Government.

> *'CODA refers to any hearing person born to one or two Deaf parents (Bishop & Hicks 2005: Bull 1998: Mand et al 2009). ... According to Bishop and Hicks (2005), The term 'CODA' is reserved for people who see themselves 'as not quite fitting into the Deaf/hearing group, it is for people who want to carve out a third niche for themselves'.*

A Bicultural and Bilingual World

I don't really agree with the second of these statements. I don't feel CODAs want to carve out a 'niche' for ourselves, it is more a way to try and describe ourselves. Incidentally, it is only recently that my siblings and I had heard the term CODA. We would sign, 'Mother Father Deaf Hearing Me' when we met new Deaf people. Sometimes, we would say to hearing people, *"Both my parents are Deaf"*, which is definitely English. Many times, when I have said or signed CODA, people ask, *"What does that mean?"* Even when I say, *"Mother Father Deaf Me Hearing."* I get the same response! Much of the time, I don't mention anything to hearing people. My siblings and I don't really like the acronym.

I have been shown four different BSL variations for CODA. My favourite is the one shown to me by a Deaf friend. To do this sign you use the first and second fingers together of your right hand and place them in the centre of your forehead then move them down to touch the top of your chest. I like the sign because it connects your head and your heart.

Sometimes I have asked myself, *"Where do I belong? Should I choose which Community I belong to?"* My siblings and I have discussed this topic. We feel as a family, living all together, we lived in a 'bubble', in an almost isolated community. Mummy went food shopping to the same shop, in Cherry Hinton Road, Cambridge; we went to Newnham for picnics, went to Deaf outing, parties and Deaf Clubs, but we didn't really go anywhere else. Was it because we were financially very poor, or because my parents only went to the places where they felt comfortable?

> *Quigley and Paul (1990) estimate that approximately 5% of CODAs are born to two Deaf parents and 10% of CODAs are born to one Deaf parent and one hearing parent.*

This was new information to me, which I found very interesting.

> *Hearing CODAs come from all ethnic, religious and economic backgrounds. The only common characteristic is having Deaf parents (Filer & Filer 2000)... Generally, they grow up as a part of the Deaf community and learn Sign Language as their first language (Bishop & Hicks 2005).*

This is somewhat true of my family, we all sign to various degrees and we all grew up as part of the Deaf community, but only three of us have continued to keep this close connection to the Deaf Community. I have met other CODAs from different backgrounds more recently but our family, and friends of our family, were all quite similar.

> *Moreover, Lane et al. (1996) assert that it is not the degree of audiological deafness that decides whether an individual is Deaf or not, but the degree of identification with the Deaf community. The deciding factor is usually 'attitudinal deafness' (Napier 2002)... Mallory, Schein, and Zingle (1992) state that 10% of Deaf people marry hearing people, and if these hearing people are fluent in Sign Language, the family language is likely to be Sign Language.*

These different family dynamics imply that children in such families will be raised in a Deaf environment, even if they are themselves hearing.

I agree with the above. I feel being CODAs does not give us 'licence' to join the Deaf Community, there are boundaries to which we have to adhere. I'm not sure I agree having one Deaf parent implies the children will be brought up in a Deaf environment, it does depend on the strength of the parent, or how committed they are to the Deaf Community, whether they sign or whether they are oral. It also a decision for each individual family and their own 'dynamics'.

'Children of Deaf Adults grow up in Deaf families, but not all CODA's grow up in a Deaf community. (Hoffmeister 2008).

This is so true. I have known a Deaf friend and his wife for years and knew their son, who is hearing. Recently they mentioned their daughter, who is also hearing. I was surprised as I had never seen their daughter at any Deaf events, or even knew they had a daughter. They told me their daughter was hearing but didn't sign or was not close with the family. I did meet their daughter once through work. She told me she didn't sign or attend Deaf events or see her parents very often, which I feel is a sad situation. Being a CODA can mean you can either get involved or opt out! Just imagine, your parents are part of a community which you don't want to be part of. Yet, to exclude yourself from that community can mean you exclude yourself from your family.

Language Brokers

> *Language brokering in Deaf-parented families arises from the fact that many Deaf adults may or may not have a reasonable ability to read and write spoken language and also may not be able to communicate adequately through spoken language (Hall & Guéry 2010). As a result, their children often act as language brokers between their Deaf parents and the hearing community (Hall & Guéry 2010). Language brokering in these families ranges from sporadic to regular, and CODAs are often forced to start language brokering from a very young age (Preston 1996). … there were no formal rules when it came to assigning the role of interpreter in the family because CODAs reported that they had had to interpret for their parents at some point in time, regardless of the CODAs' birth order or gender.*

How lucky for my parents to have ten 'language brokers' in a range of ages over a 22-year period. Gabrielle started it all when she was a little girl during the Second World War letting Mummy know when the air raid was sounding by pulling at her skirt; to Francesca, the youngest, going shopping with our parents and to the cinema, sometimes explaining what the film was about. As we got older, we all took turns, no one child was assigned to any role. If they needed someone to go with them to appointments, which was infrequent, it fell to whoever was available at the time.

My siblings and I have discussed interpreting for our parents. I like the idea of being named a 'Language

A Bicultural and Bilingual World

Broker' rather than an interpreter. There were times when we were Language Brokers for our parents in a variety of situations, like doctors, dentists, opticians etc. We all felt it was always an 'honour' and never a 'burden', to be there for our parents. We never felt 'forced'. Maybe the situation would be very different if my parents only had one or two children, having ten of us must have been a blessing for them and shared the responsibility for us, particularly between the girls.

> *Furthermore, Morales and Hanson (2005) assert that children who served as language brokers also attempted to protect their parents from negative comments or embarrassment while interpreting. In an attempt to protect their Deaf parents, children who act as language brokers may not interpret insensitive remarks made by a hearing person about the Deaf parent as the hearing person may assume that all the family members are Deaf because they are using Sign Language to communicate.*

I am guilty of this myself, not just for my parents but also for other Deaf people.

> *This study revealed that female CODAs are more likely to interpret for their families and male children are less likely to do so, which appears to correlate with other studies (Buriel et al. 1998; Love 2003; Mallory et al. 1992; Preston 1994). Also, according to Buriel et al. (1998) and Love (2003), female children are more likely to act as interpreters than male children.*

We Are CODA

I cannot comment on other families, but with our family this statement is totally accurate. The six girls were far more, and still are, fluent and had an ability to adapt to situations with language brokering. Our four brothers, never backed down from supporting our parents, they were just less fluent. At times this would frustrate Daddy. My brother Claudius, just fingerspells and it was always good enough and he still does today.

Furthermore, over and above interpreting, the CODAs in this study highlighted the importance of maintaining and facilitating communication so that there is no communication breakdown between the parties involved. Therefore, they had to facilitate communication and not simply interpret or convey what was being said. DeMent and Buriel (1999) and Tse (1995) stated that the role of interpreters is to facilitate communication between two linguistically and/ or culturally different communities, and not only conveying information, which the CODAs in this study seemed to have done. This added responsibility may place CODAs under pressure to ensure that communication is successful, even in situations that they feel are not ideal.

Wow! This was powerful stuff for me. It brought back vivid memories of Claudius communicating Daddy's diagnosis of lung cancer exchange with the doctor. He was able to facilitate information flow even if not directly interpreting.

A Bicultural and Bilingual World

At a similar time to Daddy's diagnosis, I read an article in a national newspaper, about a son who was in a similar situation to Claudius. An interpreter was not provided for him and his family, so the son sued the hospital for failing to do so as he felt he was put under great emotional pressure. I feel this man was right to take this approach, however we never felt this need: we thought it an honour to be there when we were most needed by our parents.

> An added bonus is that CODAs 'enjoy a command of the languages and the cultural knowledge of two worlds' and they benefit from that experience (Lane et al. 1996:171). Singleton and Tittle (2000) suggest that if the role of the parent is clear and the interpreting is kept to appropriate contexts, the added responsibility of interpreting can result in maturity, independence and an opportunity to have rich experiences. These authors claim that children who learn to navigate and explore the hearing world independently 'develop positive attributes such as adaptiveness, resourcefulness, curiosity and "worldliness"'

For me, this is absolutely true. I left home at sixteen, to move to London. I have travelled to many countries on my own. My thoughts have always been, if you want to do it, do it!

Language Development

My first experience at school, where I was smacked for not answering to 'Madeleine Hempstead' (as I had not heard my surname before), prompted me to research on the language development and exposure to words between Deaf parents with hearing children.

It is thought by the age of five hearing children of hearing parents should have at least two thousand words in their vocabulary, but I wonder if this would be significantly different for hearing children of Deaf parents.

I found another research paper, '*Communication problems in hearing children of Deaf parents*' (Schiff & Ventry, 1976) which studied fifty-two children of Deaf parents, who were thought to have normal hearing. These children were evaluated for speech, hearing, and language problems. Of the fifty-two hearing children, they assessed less than half were considered to be developing speech and language normally. Twelve percent had previously undiagnosed hearing loss.

I wondered if my siblings and I would have been considered as underdeveloped in speech and language.

The research also stated,

> '*The children appeared to be using two systems to communicate, one with hearing people and one with Deaf*'.

This was true of my family; we had a bilingual communication system in our house.

Then it says,

> '*However, when an elder sibling had speech and language difficulty, the younger siblings tended to have similar problems*'.

I looked at this statement in reverse. My eldest sister, Gabrielle, went to a private convent school, in

A Bicultural and Bilingual World

Cambridge, paid for by an aunt. Gabrielle speaks in a very eloquent manner, very clear and precise. She is now in her eighties and still speaks eloquently. My sisters and I tended to follow Gabrielle and developed a clear, precise speaking style. My eldest brother went to the local Roman Catholic School and spoke with more of a Cambridge accent. My brothers tended to follow him!

I find it interesting that the world of CODAs is now being explored and studied, and I love that my siblings and I have direct experience to compare to the research findings.

We Are CODA

Travelling As A CODA

My favourite past time is travelling whether it is here in the UK or abroad, but it is a very expensive hobby, especially as I prefer to travel on my own. Single travel often requires me pay a single supplement, which I feel is an unfair practice. Many people, especially women, ask me, *"Why do you travel on your own? Aren't you scared?"* My answer is always, *"When I am at home, I am someone's mother, grandmother, employee, aunt, sister and so on. When I travel by myself, I get to be me."*

I envy people who are happy and contented just to not go anywhere. Many years ago, I met an elderly lady who had lived in March, Cambridgeshire all her life and had only left the town once for her honeymoon in Blackpool! She said she had seen the world through having 'Sky' on her TV. A happy lady.

I am different, I have moved house 13 times, lived in Cambridge, London, Norfolk, Suffolk, Derbyshire, Cambridgeshire and now, Kent. My nickname with my relatives is Marco Polo, a traveller in the 13th Century, I guess he didn't stay in one place for too long either!

When I travel overseas, I try to find accommodation with a family or in a small family run hotel or bed and breakfast. I find this way I gain more local experiences rather than the usual tourist traps. Once settled in, my first outing is to find the local Deaf Community. Whether abroad or at home, I feel more comfortable amongst the Deaf Community, I'm more myself. I look forward to looking at the differences between their Deaf Community and their Sign Language to that of the UK.

Paris

My first trip abroad by plane, was a weekend away in Paris. A birthday present from my children for my 40th birthday. I clearly remember standing at the airport, with a rucksack on my back, petrified. My legs were shaking and I was sure everyone could see. However, the minute I was on the plane, that was it! I was hooked on travelling abroad.

Being on my own for the first time in a different country was so exciting: no one knew me or my background I felt such a sense of freedom. I could be whoever I want. The French were very friendly. One brassiere I went to a few times, made me a little cake with a candle on top and sang *Happy Birthday* to me.

As I pottered around Paris, enjoying my freedom, I hoped to meet some Deaf people, and I did. It was a fantastic moment for me, meeting Deaf people from another country, I knew our sign language would be different (which is the same in spoken or written English and French) but we got by on basic gestures

USA

My first long haul flight was to San Francisco to stay with one of my sisters. I really prefer long haul flights, maybe the further away from home the better. On this trip, I had no inkling I would visit the United States many times or visit fourteen States over the following twenty years.

In 2013, my son and his wife moved to New York. New York became my second home and I spent a few months a year there. It gave me an opportunity to meet Deaf American people and build a relationship with a few. During one stay, I attended the DeafNation Expo on Staten Island, and the Black Deaf Interpreters Awards in New York. Thank you again, Daddy for teaching me some basic American Signs and (ASL) and American fingerspelling.

I have also spent many months over the years in Florida, in a town named Port Charlotte, where my son's father lives. I first made enquires at the local library about the Deaf Community: they had a Deaf Church and a Deaf Club every two weeks. Armed with this information, I cycled (I relied on a bike whilst I was there), map in hand to find them. I met some wonderful Deaf people. We would spend a lot of our time discussing which signs were better BSL or ASL. There is such a huge difference in the Signs, this made us laugh so much as we got confused, even with fingerspelling!

We Are CODA

Central Americas

Whilst on a trip to Cuba, I took a three-day side trip to Montego Bay, Jamaica. It was not the safest place to visit, but I managed to find and buy a Jamaican Sign Language Book. The signs are very similar to American.

Japan

I landed at Hanela Airport and found accommodation at a lovely Japanese home. I was intrigued to find a TV channel for disabled people. I watched a documentary about a wife and husband, where the wife went to work and the husband (who was Deaf & Blind) stayed at home fending for himself. They lived in a rural location and had a large outdoor area to grow food. The husband managed the household and did the garden, cleaning, washing etc. The wife spoke to the interviewer and signed on her husband's hand what she was saying. They seemed a happy and an independent couple. I thought the channel was a great addition to the TV programming and wonder why there isn't a Disabled Channel in the UK. Then I think about Deaf friends who do not see being Deaf as a disability - would they appreciate it or enjoy it?

After watching the programme, I wondered if they had a Japanese Sign Language (JSL) book. Off I went to find a bookshop, eventually I found one (these were the days before Google™ Maps) then started the game of Charades: book, TV, pointing to my ears and shaking my head! The poor shop assistant looked at me, looking very confused. She put her hand up (I guessed she wanted me to wait) then off she went. She came back with another lady who had a badge on her lapel. I thought she could be the manager. Out came Charades again. Suddenly, she smiled and waved her hand to follow her, she walked over to a bookshelf and pointed, with a smile and a bow. I left the bookshop with my purchase of a JSL book and a smile.

Australia

While I was in Australia, I bought an Auslan (Australian Sign Language) book, which I was pleased about as Auslan Signs are very similar to British Sign Language. I had heard about the Long Bay Correctional Centre, where the infamous 'Ned Kelly' was imprisoned. I thought I would take the opportunity to visit.

When I phoned, the prison was keen for me to visit and have a look round. I was so excited; I got myself on a bus a few days later. The bus stopped outside a large 'park looking' complex. It was a long walk up a hill to get to the prison gates.

There were three guards at the gates: all with guns (unlike British prisons). I met Shirley, who managed the Disabled Prisoners' section of the prison. Disabled prisoners had their own small building on the site. She informed me most of the prisoners she supported were Aboriginals (now known as Indigenous Australians) who, when they arrived, were unable to read or write. A programme was created to support Deaf Aboriginal prisoners. Shirley said it was difficult because they did not have any structured form of Sign Language due to the way they lived within their own 'closed' community. In some ways this meant they had their own 'community signs'. The Australian Government thought it would be best for all Deaf Aboriginals prisoners complete their sentencing after they had learnt to read and write.

Shirley showed me a cupboard full of minicoms for Deaf prisoners. I was green with envy: it would have been wonderful if UK prisoners *had* had access to minicoms.

Minicoms are a Collins Dictionary device used by Deaf and hard-of-hearing people which enabled typed messages to be sent and received. It could be accessed via a normal phone line and other minicom devices. It had a small screen to display the typed text (I remember the texts were not always clear). This is because the text is transmitted live. When the hearing person's phone rang, and they picked it up and heard a whining noise, they knew it was a minicom call and put the phone receiver on the cups of the minicom. Minicom usage started to decline when the mobile phone became an easier way to communicate. Mobile phone also enable calls with many callers at one time rather than 'one person at a time' as was the case with the minicom. The mobile phone also provides greater confidentiality than the minicom.

At the time of my work within the UK Prison system, I enquired why they would not allow minicoms. I was told prison calls are monitored, and it would not be possible to monitor a minicom communication. Later models did print out conversations, as long there was a roll of paper in the minicom.

China

I left Australia and went onto Shanghai to visit a friend and her husband (they are both Chinese) who lived in a very exclusive part of Shanghai. Unfortunately, I didn't see my friend, as she had moved.

So, I settled into a small cheap hotel in Old Shanghai. At night I could see the beautiful lights of Shanghai across the Huangpu River. There were modern skyscrapers, world banks, all very different from the humble hotel in which I stayed! Going over to the 'other side', Downtown Shanghai, to me, was similar to any westernised city.

The day before I left Shanghai, I asked the hotel staff where the Deaf school was and if they could phone and ask if I could visit. The school agreed I could visit that day and off I went in a taxi.

The school was a modern building with lots of windows open and without heating; everyone wore padded clothing. My clothing was unsuitable for Shanghai November weather, I was cold.

On my arrival at the school, I was met by a very nice Chinese lady who spoke very good English, (with an American accent). She showed me around the school and took me to meet some of the older students aged 16 or 17.

The Deaf children signed in ASL while I was signed in BSL. We had a fun debate on which Sign Language was best. I tried hard to promote BSL, while they were very strongly advocating for ASL. We had a good time with lots of laughs, confusion and misunderstanding of each other signs.

I enquired why ASL was used, as I thought the children would be signing in their own Chinese Sign Language. The lady told me they were preparing for Gallaudet University in America to continue their education and to achieve a degree. I was quite surprised, but thinking about it later, if any Deaf children from England wanted to go to the only University for Deaf people, they would have to do the same and learn ASL.

In the 1970s, The World Federation for the Deaf tried to create a 'Standard International Sign Language' to make it easier for communication during meetings. A book was published with fifteen hundred signs. I would love to have a copy, if you have a spare copy please let me know.

Hong Kong

I am a bit of a foodie and had wanted to visit Hong Kong for a long time. I stayed in a small hotel which provided a bed (breakfast was extra). I was pretty excited to try the 'local cafe's food'. Sitting down in a local cafe, I discovered the menu only had Chinese characters and poor-quality photos of the food. I just pointed, not sure what I was going to eat, but I find this is half the fun!

On my second day in Hong Kong, I asked at the hotel desk if there was a Deaf Centre nearby, which there was. The concierge phoned the Centre for me to ask if I could visit, they said they would love me to pop over. I spent the rest of the day with them. Communication was bit of a struggle, but we made it through. They wanted to know if I could help them with signs for a play, they wanted someone to interpret in Chinese. This was going to be a first for them. I asked what the play was, it was '*The Vagina Monologues*'. I was stunned! Their first ever play to be signed! Impossible task, I had to say, "No."

They gave me a DVD on Hong Kong Sign Language and I gave them a book on British Sign Language. We had a lovely time together, they asked me to join them for a picnic the next day, but sadly I couldn't go as I was leaving for Vietnam.

Vietnam

I enjoy Vietnamese food and was really looking forward to this part of my trip. I stayed in a small bed and breakfast in the heart of Hanoi, it was nice and clean and I loved their summer spring rolls; in fact, I made some myself at a little cookery course just around the corner from my accommodation.

On the first morning, I wandered out doing a bit of sightseeing and found a stall where a young girl was selling homemade items, mainly bookmarks. She was holding a sign in front of her which said DEAF. We started to communicate in Sign Language, she told me about her boyfriend and asked if I would like to go the Hostel for the Deaf. The Hostel was called Deaf Craft 5 Colors and was based in a less favourable area. There was even a food stall nearby selling dog meat. I met some other residents who lived there and, of course, her boyfriend. They all lived and worked in the same room. They made crafts to sell on the streets of Hanoi.

At night they put their crafts away and unrolled mats to sleep. I wondered if they would live there until they were a certain age or got married!

I have recently looked on Tripadvisor® which mentions Deaf Craft 5 Colors. It states it 'provides employment for people in the Vietnamese community who are Deaf enabling them to live independent lives.'

Bangkok

When I arrived in Bangkok, I took an instant dislike to the place, I walked from Arrivals to Departures to ask for the next flight home. I was told there were no seats available for 36 hours. I booked there and then. While I waited, I found a bed and breakfast to rest and went to sleep.

Street of Deaf Traders

The following morning, after breakfast, I thought I would have a look around, get a map and see if I could find the street. I had not realised my accommodation was actually located on the The Street of Deaf Traders. I was happy and ready to sign. I found a Deaf tailor with his sewing machine outside a shop. He was happy when I signed, "*My Daddy tailor.*" His signs were a mixture of Thai and American. I had so much fun. I also met a Deaf artist, a Deaf baker and a Deaf souvenir shop owner. In Bangkok, many Deaf people were taught trade skills alongside their basic education in Deaf schools. For boys it was shoemaking, upholstering and tailoring and many other practical trades. For the girls, it was either dress-making, laundry, cleaning and other basic domestic tasks. They would set up stalls to ply their trade and were very popular; they were cheap but very skilled due to their apprenticeships at Deaf schools.

Turkey

While in Turkey, I met with a young Deaf man, we had a lovely time signing away. A friend I was travelling with asked how I could understand Turkish Sign Language. I didn't! It is difficult to explain but by being bi-lingual (knowing English and BSL) I find it easy to adapt and search for understanding. Sometimes it is just a matter of trying.

Ireland

I also had an opportunity to visit Dublin Deaf Centre and ended up partying at the pubs with a group of young Deaf people! The main difference between British and Irish Sign Language is Ireland has male and female signs primarily because the girls and boys went to separate schools. Most signs were created by Deaf children at Deaf schools.

Restarting after Covid

In 2023, I booked a coach trip with Newmarket Holidays. The trip covered five countries, Czech Republic, Slovakia, Austria, Germany and Hungary in eight days. I chose this trip because it meant I could add four new countries to my list of places visited.

Czech Republic

The first stop was Prague, where there was a Deaf Café. I went off to find it and have some lunch. I communicated with the staff just to order a baked camembert and a glass of water. On each table there was a small wooden stand, one half was red and the other was green. When the green half was at the top the staff knew you wanted to order. When you displayed the red half up, the staff would know when to give

you your bill. There were no Deaf customers so I didn't get to chat to anyone. After lunch, I took the metro to the city centre and found a bookshop which sold a Czech Sign Language book. I bought it to add to my collection of Sign Books from other countries.

Signal Block: Green on top

I enjoy meeting Deaf people from other countries and visiting other Deaf Clubs, just to pop in, have a chat and get to know any cultural differences. With all the Deaf Clubs I have taken myself into, not once have I been ignored or rejected. I do not feel this is because I am a CODA, but because I can communicate. You do

Deaf Cafe in Prague, October 2023

not need to be a CODA, but do need to sign fluently and be able to adapt your communication to match each individual you meet. Over my many years of travel, I have visited many Deaf Clubs and Centres. A lot of them are now closed, which is sad for the Deaf Community and me.

My Future Travels

I hope to continue my travels, in the UK and abroad, and look forward to experiencing many other wonderful encounters with Deaf people and CODAs of other nationalities.

We Are CODA

228

My First Non-Family CODA Experience

While researching for this book about the CODA film, I found information for two CODA organisations! I was stunned and could not believe such organisations existed. I asked myself, why haven't I heard of these organisations before? Here I am in my seventies, having spent my life with a feeling I didn't quite fit in within the hearing world. Most of my friends are Deaf, my social life is mostly with Deaf people and then there is my extended Deaf Family.

It never occurred to me there would be a CODA Community I could communicate with and feel comfortable! The only CODAs I have known are my own brothers and sisters and hearing children from the Deaf Club. I never needed to look outside my family, as there were nine CODAs for me to hang out with. We understand each other's sense of humour, our 'Family Signs' and our own way of communication.

Now there is a whole new world out there for me! I asked myself, *"Do I make connection? Will we have a similar communication and culture? Will they understand me and would I be welcomed? Will I feel comfortable and 'safe' to be myself?"* So many questions: I was nervous and unsure I would be accepted just because I am a CODA.

CODA International

There is a CODA International, a worldwide organisation which celebrates and supports CODAs from around the world. Recently, I was on a Zoom meeting where I was talking to people from America, Spain and Germany, I couldn't believe it! CODA International are celebrating their forty year anniversary in San Diego, America in May 2024, I had never heard of them before 2022. It just never occurred to me these groups even existed. My siblings were also surprised when I told them about the CODA organisations. Like me they had always thought there wasn't many other CODAs around, what a shock to find out that CODA International had been going for forty years and that CODAs have groups around the world.

CODA UK & Ireland

The second organisation I made contact with was CODA UK & Ireland. They are a professional organisation like CODA International. I joined and I met Matthew Shrine, their Welfare Director, via a Zoom meeting, I was anxious beforehand, but he was nice and chatty. It was obvious we had a common connection; his father is Deaf, as are other members of his family.

Matthew emailed asking if I would like to join a bunch of CODAs from CODA UK & Ireland for a weekend in Nottingham in November 2023. I had to build up

My First Non-Family CODA Experience

courage to attend the weekend. Sadly, none of my siblings were able to go, so it was just me! This was my first CODA meeting with a group of other CODAs.

I arrived at the hotel with no idea how many people would be there and who they would be! I sat in the bar on my own and waited not realising they were already in the bar and were the noisy bunch of young people in the corner. These were a young, bubbly, noisy group of people who accepted me with open arms. We chatted, signed and talked about the experiences of our Deaf parents. We also had the same sense of humour which is a mix of Deaf and CODA. There were about 28 of us; many worked as Sign Language Interpreters, Teachers of the Deaf and Care Providers for Deaf people.

How refreshing it was to see young CODAs who are so proud of being together and sharing their experiences. For the first time in my life, here were hearing people I was able to chat with about 'regional' and 'old and new signs'. Never before had I had this conversation outside the Deaf Community. I found it very emotional, in a good way. Two of the younger CODAs were grandchildren of someone I knew. It was lovely to have this link.

There is even a summer camp for CODA children, for ages 7 to 17. The last summer camp was in July 2023, when over a hundred children of Deaf parents could have fun together. There is a CODA Culture and Community out there and I am proud to be a part of this wonderful, rich bilingual and bicultural Community. I just wish I knew about this when I was younger. Maybe one day I shall take my grandchildren!

We Are CODA

I am very excited to attend the CODA UK & Ireland Conference in Cork in October 2024. I have been invited to make a presentation at the conference about my life, the book and the process of writing it. I am looking forward to meeting hundreds of people from my Culture, including CODAs and take this book with me!

My
CODA
Future

> "The limits of my language means the limits of my world."

Ludwig Wittgenstein

Where I Am Now

I was in a car crash in November 2023: the collision was not of my doing. I won't go into too many details, but a significant moment I remember is having to hold onto the steering wheel with all the strength I had while the car spun out of control. It was very scary.

This trauma of the collision has had an extremely negative effect on me, physically, emotionally and mentally: it fully effected my ability to communicate with my usual skill and expression.

After a few months, I felt ready to socialise within the Deaf Community again. How wrong I was! It was devastating. I couldn't concentrate on signing; my hand shapes were sloppy and my mind kept wondering. As I concentrated on signing, I became more worn out. I was exhausted after only a short time. I kept saying to myself, *"Concentrate, concentrate"* but I just couldn't.

When I continued to push myself to concentrate, headaches started and brain fog kicked in. Many of my Deaf friends commented on this and continually asked if I was okay and did I know what they were saying.

I lot of the time I couldn't. I was unable to communicate effectively with confidence. It was heartbreaking.

Luckily, I am now improving in concentration and able to communicate well with my Deaf friends. I still find I easily tire; mentally and physically.

My Hopes for the Future

For Hearing People: I hope my message illuminates the often-overlooked CODA community, a group which has been largely unrecognised, marginalised, and unsupported for centuries. CODAs serve as a vital link between the Deaf and hearing worlds - a bridge of untapped knowledge, awareness, and capability. Our unique versatility enables us to navigate effortlessly between these two realms, seamlessly transitioning between sign and speech. This ability allows us to foster inclusivity, ensuring that conversations between Deaf and hearing individuals are not just possible, but enriched for all involved.

For Deaf People: You may not have realised that CODAs, often the children of your friends, might feel left out or excluded from your community, leading to a potential disconnection from their own parents (especially if they are overlooked or disregarded simply because they can hear). Not all CODAs have been as fortunate as my siblings and I, who were blessed with parents who made sure we were included and felt like an integral part of the Deaf Community.

If you are Deaf, you might discover that you can form deep and meaningful friendships with CODAs. Many CODAs possess strong sign language skills and an

Where I Am Now

awareness of the issues faced by the Deaf community. Through these connections, you may find common ground and gain a deeper understanding of each other's cultures.

For fellow CODAs: I encourage you to take the time to read this book. I hope it reassures you that you are not alone - there are many other CODAs who share similar experiences and frustrations. I urge you to seek out and connect with other CODAs, build a support network for yourselves and your families. Let's support one another.

We Are CODA

Extras

We Are CODA

*"Language is not a genetic gift, it is a social gift.
Learning a new language is becoming a member of
the club - the community of speakers
of that language."*

Frank Smith

Additional Reading

There are some other books about CODAs you may want to read to gain additional perspectives. Most of them seem to come from the USA. Whilst I was doing some research I found them, I haven't read them all, yet!

Books

Preston, P., (1994), *Mother Father Deaf – Living Between Sound & Silence: Living Between Sound and Silence,* (Harvard University Press: Harvard), https://www.amazon.co.uk/Mother-Father-Deaf-Between-Silence/dp/0674587472

Sorenson, D., (2019), *Between Two Worlds – My Life as a Child of Deaf Adults,* (Gallaudet University Press), https://www.amazon.co.uk/Between-Two-Worlds-Child-Adults/dp/1944838538

Reppert, R. A., (2016), *Adventures of a CODA,* (Xulon Press) https://www.amazon.co.uk/Adventures-CODA-Ruth-Reppert/dp/1498461662

Carolan, M. & Sindorf, K., (2024), *Mom Dad Not Hear: 30 Powerful Stories and Lessons about Leadership, Life, and Love from My Deaf Parents,* (Third Culture Books) https://www.amazon.co.uk/Mom-Dad-Not-Hear-Leadership/dp/B0CT28YKG1

Walker, L.A., (1986), *A Loss for Words: The Story of Deafness in a Family,* (HarperCollins), https://www.amazon.co.uk/Loss-Words-Story-Deafness-Family/dp/0060156449

Napier, J., (2021), *Sign Language Brokering in Deaf-Hearing Families,* (Palgrave Macmillan), https://www.amazon.co.uk/Sign-Language-Brokering-Deaf-Hearing-Families/dp/3030671399

We Are CODA

Sidransky, R., (1992), *In Silence: Growing Up Hearing in a Deaf World*, (Piatkus Books), https://www.amazon.co.uk/Silence-Growing-Hearing-Deaf-World/dp/0749910984

Miller, R.H., (2004), *Deaf Hearing Boy – A Memoir: A Memoir Volume 2 (Deaf Lives)*, (Gallaudet University Press), https://www.amazon.co.uk/Deaf-Hearing-Boy-Memoir-Lives/dp/1563683059/

Journal Articles

Harrison, J. & Watermeyer, B., 2019, '*Views from the borderline: Extracts from my life as a coloured child of Deaf adults, growing up in apartheid South Africa*', African Journal of Dis-ability 8(0), a473. https://doi.org/10.4102/ajod.v8i0.473, https://www.ncbi.nlm.nih.gov/pmc/articles/PMC5968869/#:~:text=Globally%2C%20it%20is%20suggested%20that,2009), 15/07/2024

References

Throughout the book I have referred to certain papers or books. Here are their citations should you wish to further your reading on them.

Journals

Moroe NF, and de Andrade V., (2018), *Hearing children of Deaf parents: Gender and birth order in the delegation of the interpreter role in culturally Deaf families. Afr J Disabil. 2018 Apr 30;7:365. doi: 10.4102/ajod.v7i0.365. PMID: 29850437; PMCID: PMC5968869.

Heffernan, G. & Nixon, E., (2023), *Experiences of Hearing Children of Deaf Parents in Ireland*, Journal of Deaf Studies and Deaf Education, 28, 399-407, https://doi.org/10.1093/deafed/enad018 https://www.ncbi.nlm.nih.gov/pmc/articles/PMC10516342/ 15/07/2024

Inclusion London, (2024), *The Cultural Model of Deafness, Inclusion London*, London, https://www.inclusionlondon.org.uk/about-us/disability-in-london/cultural-model-of-deafness/the-cultural-model-of-deafness/#:~:text=The%20Cultural%20Model%20of%20Deafness%20explains%20the%20position%20of%20the,has%20within%20the%20Deaf%2-0community. 15/07/2024

Editors, The, (2024), *British Sign Language – A language of the UK*, Government Communication Service, https://gcs.civilservice.gov.uk/news/the-gcs-has-published-guidance-for-members-on-how-to-plan-for-and-produce-british-sign-language-bsl-content/#:~:text=Sign%20Language%20Week%20(18%20to,government%20on%2018%20March%202003. 15/07/2024

Peabody, A., (2021), *Education for Deaf Prisoners*, Written Evidence, UK Parliaments, https://committees.parliament.uk/work/817/prison-education/publications/written-evidence/?page=3 22/08/2024

We Are CODA

Schiff N.B., & Ventry I.M., *Communication problems in hearing children of deaf parents,* J Speech Hear Disord. 1976 Aug;41(3):348-58. doi: 10.1044/jshd.4103.348. PMID: 950794. https://pubmed.ncbi.nlm.nih.gov/950794/ 05/08/2024

Editors, The, (1939), *Scheme to Warn Deaf of Night Air Raid,* The British Deaf Times, Edition Unknown, p90.

Books

Moore, T. Captain Sir, (2020), *Tomorrow Will Be A Good Day,* Charnwood: Leicester

Murray, A., Depledge, I., Urquhart. I. and Webb, D. (Eds), (2015), *A Pictorial History of the British Deaf Association 1890-2015,* British Deaf History Society Publications: Glasgow

Sacks, O., (2009), *Seeing Voices,* Picador: London

Films, Musicals and TV

14 Days in May, (1987), **Paul Hamann,** BBC: London

Godspell, (1971), **Schwartz S., & Tebelak,** M. Off-Broadway: New York

Sunshine on Leith, (2007) **Greenhorn, S.,** (featuring songs of **The Proclaimers**), Dundee Rep Theatre: Scotland

The Song of Bernadette, (1943), **Henry King,** 20th Century Fox: Los Angeles

Websites

Berke, J., (2023), *The Milan Conference of 1880: When Sign Language Was Almost Destroyed,* Very Well Health, https://www.verywellhealth.com/Deaf-history-milan-1880-1046547 23/09/2024

Editors, The, (2024), *Irish Names,* Behind the Name, https://www.behindthename.com/names/usage/irish 24/09/2024

Editors, The, (2024), *CODA Quotes,* IMDb, https://www.imdb.com/title/tt10366460/quotes/ 23/09/2024

Editors, The, (2024), *William Sidney HEMPSTEAD,* Deaflympics, https://deaflympics.com/athletes/william-hempstead 22/08/2024

Ellis, M., (2022), *What Is Syntax? Learn the Meaning and Rules, With Examples,* Grammarly, https://www.grammarly.com/blog/syntax/ 23/09/2024

References

Kelly, N., (2011), *Meet Jack Jason: The Most Famous Interpreter in the World,* Huffpost, https://www.huffpost.com/entry/meet-jack-jason-the-most_b_901712 23/09/2024

Maya-Martinez, M., (2022) *Welsh language: A national treasure,* Civil Service, https://civilservice.blog.gov.uk/2022/07/19/welsh-language-a-national-treasure/ 23/09/2024

McGoey, A., (2020), *What it is like being a hearing child of deaf parents,* Hearing Like Me, https://www.hearinglikeme.com/being-a-hearing-child-of-deaf-parents/#:~:text=I%20sincerely%20wish%20that%20people,it%20will%20make%20their%20day 18/09/2024

Shah, D., (2022) *Dee's CODA Stories: The Deaf Parents,* CODA UK & Ireland, https://www.codaukireland.co.uk/post/dee-s-coda-stories-the-deaf-parents 23/09/2024

Shondas, The, (2024), *Our 20 top quotes about language learning,* Learn a Language, https://www.lcs-school.com/post/our-20-top-quotes-about-language-learning 23/09/2024

Wittgenstein, L., (2024) *16 Inspirational Quotes About Language,* Text Appeal, https://textappeal.com/cultureshocks/16-inspirational-quotes-about-language/ 23/02024

We Are CODA

"Sign language is my first language. English and Spanish are my second languages. I learned Spanish from my grandparents, sign language from my parents, and English from television."

Jack Jason, Interpreter

Appendices

We Are CODA

Appendix 1

This is the report I wrote to provide evidence to the UK government about the lack of support for Deaf prisoners.

Education for Deaf Prisoners

There have been many published reports about Deaf prisoners. None mention how 'Education in Prison', is limited / non-existence for Deaf prisoners.

My journey of supporting prisoners started from watching the documentary *14 Days in May*, (1987), a documentary about prisoners on Death Row in the United States of America. From this I became involved in a group that wrote to prisoners that were waiting to be executed.

A few years on there was an article regarding Deaf prisoners in the UK that were serving a 'Double Sentence'. (1998/99). Not only were Deaf prisoners, doing 'time' they were also being isolated from the Deaf Community (no or little communication using British Sign Language, BSL).

In 2000, the Birmingham Institute for the Deaf (known as BID) received government funding to set up

248

Appendix 1 - Education for Deaf Prisoners

the 'Deaf Prison Project' (DPP). Volunteers/Advocates were trained and vetted to work with Deaf prisoners, covering prisons in England. This role also took me to visiting prisons abroad, at my own costs. The project was funded for ten years. During this time I supported prisoners in fourteen prisons, covering parole hearings, advocacy, attending appointments within the prison, liaising with the prisoners family, solicitors, social services and probation officers. Prisoners were supported after they were released.

Deaf prisoners, should attend courses/training as part of their rehabilitation programme (especially, sex offenders training and anger management).

These courses/training were not offered to Deaf prisoners. When prison staff knew they would have to 'pay' for a communicator, it was always decided that the Deaf prisoner did not need to attend any of the courses or training!

Deaf prisoners were worried and would ask me why they can't attend the courses/ training because they were told they would have to attend before they were released! When I asked the staff why, I just got excuses, 'don't have time, prisoner does not need to attend, courses/training had been cancelled' and so on.

Deaf prisoners not only missed out on these important sessions, they also missed out on classroom education, Communication Support Workers (CSW) are used in colleges. Why does the Deaf prisoner miss out time and time again due to lack of access to a CSW. Why is never budgeted for! Each college that supplies education should have in their budget, costs for a CSW, which can cost between £10 - £20 per hour. Right to Education/Equality and Human Rights Commission states 'No person shall be denied a right to education'.

January 2021

Written evidence submitted by Agatha Peabody

Appendix 2
British Sign Language
Fingerspelling Alphabet

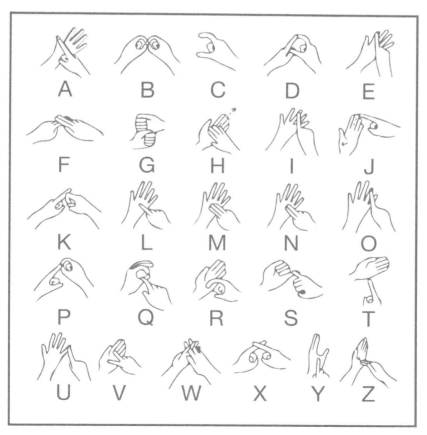

We Are CODA

"Sign language is the equal of speech, lending itself equally to the rigorous and the poetic, to philosophical analysis or to making love."

Oliver Sacks

Acknowledgements

I have a long list of people and organisations I wish to thank for helping make this book possible.

🖐 Firstly, many thanks to the brothers and sisters who have contributed to this book, without them this book would not have had so much depth and richness.

🖐 Many thanks to my children, Sebastian and Dominique, and their families, Rachel, Richard, Theodore, Tilda, Etta, Luella and Rosie.

🖐 My wonderful extended family, Will, Tora, Charlotte and Dashiell. My darling and wonderful granddaughter Bella and her sister Kim.

🖐 My cousins, Paul, Stewart, Grainne, Paul Sib, whom I have grown up with and spent many happy holidays in Cromer, Norfolk. Also my cousin Beryl.

🖐 My aunts, nieces and nephews, Simon, Nickolas, Greg, Michelle, Rachael, Simon H, James, Fiona, Helen, Justine, Alexandra, Janelle, Verity, Kellie, George, William and, of course, my dear Auntie Maureen.

🖐 Beryl - my 'hedge-walking' friend.

🖐 Deaf friends whom have known me over the years and have put up with me. These have a special mention as they are very close to my heart - Janice Silo, Nick Browne, Dianne and Loraine, Mary Moho and, of course, Ken Brewster.

"Although he was working full-time, my father involved me whenever he could in the company and always took me to be his ears at the auction sales he attended to buy parts and vehicles. I'd listen to the bidding and place his for him when he was ready."

Captain Sir Tom Moore

Acknowledgements

My Deaf friends and family from Deaf organisations which have had a positive impact in my life. Peterborough Deaf Centre, Cambridge Deaf Centre, Margate Deaf Centre, Bury St Edmunds Deaf Centre, Norwich Deaf Centre, Ipswich Deaf Centre and Birmingham Deaf Culture Centre, The Royal School for the Deaf Derby, The Royal School for the Deaf, Margate (now closed).

Deaf Club in Port Charlotte, Florida where I spent many hours trying to learn ASL (American Sign Language). My Deaf friends in New York, whom I had lots of giggles with.

Sadly, there is a RIP (Rest In Peace) for loved ones that have passed away.

My wonderful, kind and funny parents Eileen and William Hempstead, without them I would definitely not be as 'nutty' as I am. They gave me such a vibrant and loving life within such a beautiful Deaf Community/Family.

My dear nephew Christopher, who left too early, he is sadly missed.

My aunties, Yvonne, Josette, Pauline, Nora and Violet.

Allan who was a very important part of my life.

Vivian Wong who sadly died suddenly in August 2016. We were friends for 50 years, shared flats together and mixed within the London scene. She taught me all about life in London in the 1960s. That is another book! Without her I would not have had the experiences of life which was part of shaping me at a very young age.

Diane, my best friend, who stood by me and with me for more than 40 years. She knew all my secrets my life, my loves and my hates. She suddenly died November 1999 which ripped my life apart. To Diane Hall, (nee O'Brien) my soul friend, I miss you always.

My Deaf brother and sister, Billy Evans and Linda Fincham.

Paul Sibellas, my wonderful cousin. I am glad he was able to see this book and be part of it.

We Are CODA

Index

Symbols

14 Days in May 192, 248

A

Adey, Abbirose ii, xv
Adey, Ladey xi, xvi
Alderman, Neil J Dr ix
Amazon ii
American Sign Language xxi, 184,
   185, 217, 221, 222, 255
Australian Sign Language 9, 196, 219
Australian Sign Language
      Interpreters' Association
      196
Ayling-Ellis, Rose xviii

B

Bell, Alexander Graham xii
Birmingham Institute for the Deaf
      193, 248
Black Deaf Interpreters Awards
      217
British Deaf Association 46, 61, 121
British Deaf Times, The 27
British Sign Language xii, xviii, 3, 19,
      48, 51, 71, 104, 105, 133, 139,
      155, 163, 176, 177, 178, 183,
      184, 185, 187, 188, 192, 195,
      196, 197, 198, 199, 203, 204,
      205, 217, 219, 221, 223, 225,
      248, 251
Brown, Roy 81
Browne, Nick 187

Bury St Edmunds Deaf and Hard of
      Hearing Association 48

C

Cambridge Deaf Association 39, 68,
      115, 133
   History Society 39, 133
Cambridge Deaf Club ix, 25, 40, 46,
      68, 88, 133, 134, 139
Canterbury Diocesan Association
      For The Deaf 195
Children of a Lesser God xvii
Chinese Sign Language 222
Coca-Cola 138
Cochlear Implant 4
CODA International 199, 201, 230
CODA: The Film xvii, 148
CODA UK & Ireland 199, 201, 230,
      232
Columbia Pictures
   Emmanuelle 11
Co-op 26, 105, 107
Coronation Street 133
CRUSE Bereavement Support xiv
Czech Sign Language 226

D

Deaf Craft 5 Colors 223, 224
DeafNation 217
Deaf Olympics 26, 61, 116, 117, 118,
      119
Deaf Prison Project 193, 249
Deaf Together xx

257

We Are CODA

Dementia 88, 90, 91, 92, 140
  Alzheimer's Disease 89, 90, 92
Disability Discrimination Act xiii
Donovan, Jason 160
Dr. I. King Jordan 184
Dublin Deaf Centre 225
Durant, Daniel xviii

E
Eastenders xviii
Ellington, David xviii

F
Fincham, Dorothy 87, 132
Fincham House 68, 134
Fincham, John 61, 133
Fincham, Linda xi, 32, 68, 132, 185
Fincham, William 81

G
Gallaudet University 184, 222
  Gallaudet, Edward 184
Game of Thrones xix
  Stark, Benjen xix
Gap Band, The
  Oops Upside Your Head 43
Godspell xv
Granta Swimming Club 107, 116, 119

H
Hall, Diane 54
Hare, Mary Adelaide 183
Hay, John 61, 116
Heder, Sian xvii
Hepworth 38
Home-Start Brent 189
Hong Kong Sign Language 223
Human Rights Commission 194
Hunt, Arthur 62
Hunt, Irene 32, 62, 85, 132

I
Interpreting Standards of Conduct xix
Irish Sign Language 225

J
Jamaican Sign Language 218
James, Etta 10
Japanese Sign Language 218
Jason, Jack 246
Johnson, Austin 182
Jones, Emilia xvii, xxi
Jordan, I King, Dr 184

K
Kelly, Ned 219
King Henry VIII xiii
King, Stephen
  IT 138
Knox, Barbara 133
Kotsur, Troy xvii, xvii–xxii

L
Ladd, Dr Paddy 3
Language Broker 208
Lynch, Susan xix

M
Macmillan Cancer Support 122
Mary Hare Grammar School 183, 271
Matlin, Marlee xvii
Mawle, Joseph xix
McGoey, Ashley 182
Minicom 220
Minogue, Kylie 160
Missionary for the Deaf 150, 151, 152
Moore, Tom, Captain Sir 254
Mothers' Union 46

N
National Health Service 29
National Registers of
  Communication
  Professionals 195
Neighbours 160
Nurse Dorrington 82

O
Oak Lodge School, Balham 79

Index

P
Papworth Trust 191, 192
  Our Voice 191
Peabody, Agatha 250
Pernice, Giovanni xviii
Polo, Marco 215
Prince of Wales 108

Q
Queen Elizabeth II xiv, 107, 138
Queen Victoria 81

R
Radionic Hearing Aids 154
Rangammal Memorial School 187
Rossi, Jackie xvii
Rossi, Leo xviii, 148
Rossi, Ruby xvii, xxi
Rowland, Harry ix, 61
Royal National Institute for Deaf
    People xi
Royal School for Deaf Children,
    Margate ix, 41, 62, 102, 105,
    132
Royal School for the Deaf, Derby 8,
    95, 185, 186, 187, 189
Ryder, Chris ii

S
Sacks, Oliver 252
Shah, Diksha 126
Shepherd, Dr 83
Shrine, Matthew 230
Silo, Janice 186, 271
Silver Cross 114
Singer 139
Sky 215
Smith, Frank 240
Song of Bernadette, The 14
Soubirous, Bernadette 14
Soundproof xviii, xix
Spring Awakening xviii
Standard International Sign
    Language 222
Stiefel, Moritz xviii
Stork 141
Street of Deaf Traders 224

Strictly Come Dancing xviii
Sundance Film Festival xvii
Sunshine on Leith xv
Swallowe, Mr 62, 121
Sydney Deaf Club 9

T
The Rock, Cambridge 90, 113
The Rolling Stones 94
The World Federation for the Deaf
    222
Turkish Sign Language 225
Tweets, The
    The Birdie Song 43

V
Vagina Monologues, The 223
Vaseline 87

W
Welsh xiii
WhatsApp 39
Whitechapel Gallery 73
Whittingham, Dean xix
Wittgenstein, Ludwig 234
Wong, Vivian 55

Y
YouTube 1

259

We Are CODA

Notes

If you are reading this book and would like to share your thoughts on my story, please use these pages to write any notes. If you have your own CODA story or a story about Deaf Culture or the Deaf Community you would like to share with me this is also a great place to note them down. Thank you. *Madeleine*

We Are CODA

Notes

We Are CODA

Notes

We Are CODA

Notes

We Are CODA

Notes

We Are CODA

Endorsements

"It is brilliant how this book shows how Madeleine's unique upbringing as a CODA has helped her to navigate within the Deaf culture."

Mary Stanley, Alumni of Mary Hare Grammar School

"Madeleine's book shows great wisdom and a broad knowledge of CODAs, Deaf people and Deaf life. I will be reading it again and again!"

Janice Silo, Deaf Teacher (retired)

We Are CODA

www.ingramcontent.com/pod-product-compliance
Ingram Content Group UK Ltd.
Pitfield, Milton Keynes, MK11 3LW, UK
UKHW050506161224
452449UK00003BA/20